What Is Metaphysics?

Global Philosophy

Series Editor—Mohammed Rustom,
Carleton University / Tokat Institute for Advanced Islamic Studies

Given the tremendous amount of interest in non-Western philosophy today, teachers, students, and the general public are beginning to come away with a clearer picture of what "philosophy" means in various civilizations and to large sectors of humanity beyond the Anglo-American and European worlds. This series in global philosophy seeks to further this interest by highlighting the epistemic diversity and profound insights of Africana, Buddhist, Confucian, Hindu, Islamic, Jain, Jewish, Latin American, Mesoamerican, Native American, Russian, and Taoist philosophy. To accomplish its goals, the series focuses on publishing accessible and lively books on these philosophical traditions and scholarly translations of their key works.

PUBLISHED

A Sourcebook in Global Philosophy
Edited by Mohammed Rustom

Exploring Hindu Philosophy
Ankur Barua

FORTHCOMING

Exploring Africana Philosophy
Oludamini Ogunnaike

Exploring Buddhist Philosophy
Alexandra S. Ilieva

Exploring Islamic Philosophy
Sayeh Meisami

Sacred Psychology: A Global Perspective
Samuel Bendeck Sotillos

What Is Metaphysics?

Ruminations on Principial Knowledge and Some of Its Applications

SEYYED HOSSEIN NASR

equinox

SHEFFIELD UK BRISTOL CT

Published by Equinox Publishing Ltd.

UK: Office 415, The Workstation, 15 Paternoster Row, Sheffield, South Yorkshire S1 2BX

USA: ISD, 70 Enterprise Drive, Bristol, CT 06010

www.equinoxpub.com

First published 2025

© Seyyed Hossein Nasr 2025

All rights reserved. No part of this publication may be reproduced or transmitted in any form or by any means, electronic or mechanical, including photocopying, recording or any information storage or retrieval system, without prior permission in writing from the publishers.

British Library Cataloguing-in-Publication Data

A catalogue record for this book is available from the British Library.

ISBN-13	978 1 80050 647 3	(hardback)
	978 1 80050 648 0	(paperback)
	978 1 80050 649 7	(ePDF)
	978 1 80050 709 8	(ePub)

Library of Congress Cataloging-in-Publication Data

Names: Nasr, Seyyed Hossein, author.
Title: What is metaphysics? : ruminations on principial knowledge and some of its applications / Seyyed Hossein Nasr.
Description: Sheffield, South Yorkshire ; Bristol, CT : Equinox Publishing Ltd, 2025. | Series: Global philosophy | Includes bibliographical references and index. | Summary: "What is Metaphysics? offers an exposition, informed primarily by the Islamic metaphysical tradition, of principial and divine knowledge as distinct from information or merely factual knowledge. Advancing an argument in favor of integrating metaphysics at every level of one's being, the book also delves into various applications of metaphysics pertaining to the domains of religion, education, philosophy, art, ecology, and science"-- Provided by publisher.
Identifiers: LCCN 2025001309 (print) | LCCN 2025001310 (ebook) | ISBN 9781800506473 (hardback) | ISBN 9781800506480 (paperback) | ISBN 9781800506497 (pdf) | ISBN 9781800507098 (epub)
Subjects: LCSH: Metaphysics.
Classification: LCC BD111 .N375 2025 (print) | LCC BD111 (ebook) | DDC 110--dc23/eng/20250310
LC record available at https://lccn.loc.gov/2025001309
LC ebook record available at https://lccn.loc.gov/2025001310

All Scripture quotations are from the King James Version.

Typeset by Scribe Inc.

Contents

Series Foreword

Given the tremendous amount of interest in non-Western philosophy today, teachers, students, and the general public are beginning to come away with a clearer picture of what "philosophy" means in various civilizations and to large sectors of humanity beyond the Anglo-American and European worlds. This series in Global Philosophy seeks to further this interest by highlighting the epistemic diversity and profound insights of Africana, Buddhist, Confucian, Hindu, Islamic, Jain, Jewish, Latin American, Mesoamerican, Native American, Russian, and Taoist philosophy. To accomplish its goals, the series focuses on publishing accessible and lively books on these philosophical traditions, as well as scholarly translations of their key works.

Mohammed Rustom
Series Editor, *Global Philosophy*
Carleton University / Tokat Institute for Advanced Islamic Studies

Preface

The three essays that constitute this book are the result of three lectures that I delivered in Toronto, Canada, in 2015 at the Knowledge Retreat held as part of the Reviving the Islamic Spirit annual conference, in whose gatherings I participated regularly for several years. Shaykh Hamza Yusuf, who was one of the main organizers of these events and a longtime close friend of mine, asked me to devote a series of lectures to the subject of metaphysics. It was an invitation that I could not refuse. Nor could I turn down his request to prepare the text for publication. And so, after finishing several projects at hand, I turned to this work and transformed it into a written text as opposed to being only the transcription of an oral presentation. I have, however, sought to preserve some of the characteristics of an oral presentation in order to remain faithful to the lectures' original nature. Hence, I have for the most part avoided footnotes and scholarly references but have added a bibliography.

In any case, this work owes its existence to Shaykh Hamza Yusuf. In this brief note, I wish to thank him as well as Dr. Munjed Murad, Dr. Nicholas Boylston, and Ms. Katherine O'Brien, all of whom have helped me in one way or another in the preparation of this manuscript.

In conclusion, it should be stated that although the lectures that comprise this book were delivered originally to an almost completely Muslim audience—and therefore, most references are to the Islamic tradition—the work is addressed not only to Muslims but rather to all those who are interested in principial knowledge and metaphysics in the most universal sense and in the application of metaphysical principles to various realms of life and thought.

And God knows best (*wa'Llāhu a'lamu bi'l-ṣawāb*).

Seyyed Hossein Nasr
The George Washington University

Where Is Sophia?

I search here and yonder in the yesterdays and todays;
Where is that celestial Sophia to caress and embrace,
To have Her quench my thirst for philosophia prima,
The wisdom that always was, is and will be,
To be extinguished in Her arms where all answers are found?

Who am I? From where come I? Where am I going?
And yes, where should *I be going? Why am I here?*
What is the Origin? What is the End? Where is the path?
I seek with all my being, with my eye and ear,
With my imagination and reason,
With my intellect and heart.
O Sophia, I call upon Thee for help.
I call and call, but no response;
Yet, I cease not and call again.

Suddenly, Her celestial voice answers:
Seek what thou seekest within thyself.
Open the Eye of thy heart, enter thy heart, enter thy heart.
I am here to help thee if thou art earnest.

Supreme knowledge is to be found therein;
For the heart is the Throne of the Compassionate.
Thou shalt find me there, ready to embrace thee.

Seyyed Hossein Nasr
'Āshūrā', 1444 AH

1

What Is the Meaning of Metaphysics and What Is Its Significance?

Today we begin the first of three sessions in which we shall have an in-depth discussion of various aspects of metaphysics and their applications for us here today. To impress upon you what a rare occasion this is for me, let me say that I have been teaching and lecturing for many decades in various universities throughout the world, and during those many years, I have never before given a series of public lectures devoted solely to metaphysics and its applications. The teachings I have given in this field have always been private, for a few gifted students only. But one irregularity deserves another. The conditions of our times now require dissemination to the many of the knowledge that was for the few in days gone by. In any case, given the nature of the subject matter of these lectures, it is imperative to recognize that a true comprehension of them will depend on first understanding certain key ideas and concepts, many now forgotten, that I shall lay out before you.

First of all, it must be understood that an authentic presentation in written form of pure metaphysics in its traditional sense, and not as a branch of rational philosophy, has not been common in the West, nor was it ever ordinary in Islamic civilization. When such works were produced, they were meant for a few, not for ordinary readers, and were usually accompanied by oral teachings. Students and seekers who were capable of understanding such matters were first trained spiritually and intellectually for years and even decades before they were taught pure *maʿrifah*—that is, metaphysics, or pure Divine Knowledge. We live, however, in irregular times, and this irregularity requires exposing openly esoteric and metaphysical teachings; hence the appearance of traditional expositions of authentic metaphysics such as "Oriental Metaphysics" by René Guénon (d. 1951), a French Muslim metaphysician.[1] Prior to today, I myself did not accept requests to discuss pure metaphysics in depth with an audience whose members I did not know personally. When it came to teaching metaphysics to qualified students that I have had over the years, it was done on a personal and often individual level.

In today's world, however, access to the inner teachings of religion and authentic metaphysics, which is a sacred science, becomes more and more difficult every day, even in the Islamic or other Oriental civilizations whose intellectual dimensions have been better preserved than in the Christian West. We see all around us these days that outwardness and superficiality are often emphasized above inwardness and interiority, and that extends to the teaching of religion and prime philosophy themselves. Tragically, knowledge, in the sense that the Prophet (*ʿalayhiʾl-ṣalātu waʾl-salām*) taught us, is denigrated in favor of information and merely factual knowledge. Education focuses increasingly on the technological training that it values above other disciplines, while principial knowledge, knowledge of the Divine Realities, is gradually becoming eclipsed. And so, in such a situation, when an opportunity such as the one we have today arises, I think one has to break with the restrictions of the past and try to present metaphysics and gnosis in their essential reality even when one does not know everyone in the audience being addressed.

To carry out this task, we need first of all a basic understanding of what metaphysics in fact is. In a sense, metaphysics, as I am going to be using the term that I shall define in a moment, is like the fruit of a tree. From the ripe fruit, you may take a seed and plant that seed in the earth. Before long, a shoot comes up. You water it, and gradually the shoot grows into a small tree that gives first leaves and then flowers. Finally, after some time, this tree that you planted as a small seed bears fruit that in turn contains within itself the very seed that you first planted. This cycle is used as a well-known Sufi allegory. The first seed symbolizes theoretical metaphysics, theoretical knowledge of principles, but realized knowledge is in that second seed, in the fruit of that tree, the fruit that one consumes and is thus made part of one's being. In the Islamic tradition, authentic metaphysics was never taught as only cerebral knowledge; it was taught as a knowledge that is sacred and that illuminates

1. René Guénon, "Oriental Metaphysics," in *Light from the East: Eastern Wisdom for the Modern West*, ed. Harry Oldmeadow (Bloomington, IN: World Wisdom, 2007), 8–22.

us, that integrates our being, and that allows us to know who we are. This is a knowledge that not only is mental but transforms our whole being.

To delve into this issue, we must first ask ourselves, Who are we? We are both everything and nothing; that is to say, before God we are nothing, but in our heart resides the Divine Throne, the Throne of the Compassionate—*qalbu'l-mu'min 'arshu'l-Raḥmān* (The heart of the believer is the Throne of the Compassionate)—and so from that point of view, our heart contains everything. In that Center, we are everything. To realize this simultaneous everythingness and nothingness is the goal of authentic metaphysics and gnosis, and the path to that goal is one of attaining principial knowledge, of *ma'rifah* or *'ilm* in its highest sense according to the Quran. This knowledge is not to be confused with information—knowledge is not just information. What we are speaking of here is a knowledge that wounds the soul and, in doing so, transforms it. In the transformative, penetrating, shattering nature of this knowledge lies the reason why it is not meant for everyone and also why without it, a civilization dies.

What happened to Christianity in the West in modern times was that gradually, metaphysics and gnosis began to be lost and at best reduced to a branch of rational philosophy. Once they were cast aside and forgotten, theology could not defend the faith fully by itself. From the Renaissance onward in Western society, there has been a gradual erosion or lessening of the presence of the intellectual aspect of Christianity, which was the first great religion among those still extant to lose—if not totally, then at least almost totally—its metaphysical dimension. I am not speaking here about what is called metaphysics in Western philosophy; I am speaking about traditional Christian metaphysics. As a result of this weakening, Christianity could no longer produce a Saint Bonaventure (d. 1274), a Dante (d. 1321), or a Nicholas of Cusa (d. 1464). This loss is far from insignificant because metaphysics is the underpinning of every religion. No religion exists in the world in which all its adherents are metaphysicians; on the contrary, few are. But it is imperative that metaphysics exist in its essential role among the spiritual and intellectual elites because within a religious community, there are always those who ask the fundamental questions: Why? Why are things as they are? Once a religion is no longer able to answer such questions in depth for its followers, those questioners seek answers elsewhere, often outside the religious realm.

This inability to provide metaphysically satisfactory responses to profound questions is exactly the problem that arose in the modern Christian West. And such a situation is also happening to some extent in the Islamic world today, where we see members of some groups, especially among intelligent young Muslims, losing their faith because of a lack of access to the treasury of metaphysical knowledge that could respond to their calls for answers to profound existential and intellectual questions.

In the contemporary Islamic context, when a young person is seeking answers to basic questions about the nature of reality, he or she may turn to the local religious scholar or imam. Unfortunately, that religious authority may not, and often does not, have the answers. Five hundred years ago, there would have been traditional philosophers, Sufi shaykhs, or religious luminaries such as al-Ghazzālī (d. 505/1111) to respond to them. But alas, there are fewer such figures today. That young person will likely be told to stop being so inquisitive or to read the Quran more diligently. If neither of these courses of action proves fruitful—as is often the case—gradually the person falls into a state of doubt, and one of two things occurs: either he or she becomes a modernist, a person whose religious beliefs are diluted to fit the times, or that person stops asking the questions that had arisen from the depths of their soul and becomes a pure exoterist, someone who sees only the external aspects of religion. This latter view oftentimes leads to anger and frustration and even sometimes aggression and some form of fundamentalism. We certainly have seen enough of that phenomenon in our world.

Many of the people today who carry out aggressive or violent acts—sometimes even in the name of Islam—are people who at a particular moment in their life needed to have certain questions answered that were not answered for them. And so we see that metaphysics is not superfluous, not an indulgence or luxury for the philosophically inclined; it is a sine qua non, a necessity for any living religion. Any religion from which the sapiential aspect, the aspect of authentic knowledge, more or less disappears gradually becomes a shell of its former self and either decays or dies. Alas, we have had plenty of cases of this phenomenon throughout human history and especially in the modern period.

Given the critical importance of this subject, what I am going to try to do in this lecture is, first of all, provide an understanding of what real metaphysics is, what the pretensions to metaphysics have been, and what this basic issue entails. To understand metaphysics fully, one has not only to grasp it fully intellectually but also to "become" the truths with which it deals. In this work, I shall be concerned primarily with the science of metaphysics and its proper relation to other Islamic intellectual disciplines and practices.

Let us start with the term *metaphysics* itself. Some traditionalist writers have already pointed out that the word *metaphysics* in European languages, going back to Aristotle, is an unfortunate and inappropriate expression because it puts this central knowledge somewhere "out there" on the periphery. The Greek prefix, *meta*, means both "after" and "beyond." In fact, the use of the term *metaphysics* began following the circulation of a book written by Aristotle in the fourth century BC entitled *Metaphysica*—that is, the book to be read after his *Physica*.[2] In the former work, especially the book *Lambda*, major metaphysical questions are discussed, such as "What is being?" and "What is it that is the foundation of all things?" All basic questions about the nature of reality come back to these queries, since there is a presumption of being in every principial question that usually begins with "What is." In the book *Lambda*, Aristotle also turns to other important metaphysical issues, including how knowledge is possible and what the root of knowledge is, as well as other similar matters to which I shall turn later. And so this book of Aristotle made the term *metaphysics* famous in Greek, and since the book called *Metaphysica* dealt with these issues, the subject itself came to be known as metaphysics, and the word came from the Greek into Arabic, Persian, and various European languages. I need to add here that it has been pointed out by some traditionalist writers that to resuscitate the real meaning of metaphysics as *philosophia prima*, one should use it in the singular—that is, *metaphysic*—and not the plural because there is ultimately but *one* supreme science of the Real. In Islam, we use such terms as *ḥikmah* and *maʿrifah* in the singular and not plural when referring to supreme knowledge.

For a whole century, from the second to the third Islamic centuries, Islamic translators and philosophers—even al-Kindī (d. ca. 265/870), considered to be the first major Islamic philosopher and one who himself wrote a treatise on metaphysics—were concerned with how to translate the term *metaphysics* into Arabic. Should it be *mā baʿd al-ṭabīʿah*, *mā fawq al-ṭabīʿah*, or something else? Finally, after a whole century of debate, a consensus was reached, and it came to be translated as *mā baʿd al-ṭabīʿah*. *Ṭabīʿah* is used as the translation for *physikē* in Greek and *physica* in Latin, by which Aristotle's *Physics* came to be generally known. The word *physics*, based on Greek and Latin, not as understood in the modern sense, became *ṭabīʿah* and of course *mā*, meaning "what," and *baʿd*, meaning "coming after," in the Arabic rendering of the word *metaphysics*. Muslims went back to the original meaning of *metaphysikē* or *metaphysica* in Aristotle—that is, not "above" but "after" physics. Hence the term came to be known as *mā baʿd al-ṭabīʿah* in Arabic and was used extensively by the Islamic Peripatetic philosophers, such as al-Fārābī (d. 339/950) and Ibn Sīnā (d. 428/1037) or Avicenna, who were trying to Islamicize Aristotelianism and Neoplatonism and in fact succeeded

2. Alexander of Aphrodisias, who collected the works of Aristotle, used the title *Ta Meta ta Physika*, but the work has been known in the West by its Latin title, *Metaphysica*.

in doing so. The Arabic term became common, but it had a very different meaning in Islam than it has had in the West, and that difference affected, to a large extent, the trajectory of these two civilizations. In the Islamic world, the Sufis, gnostics, and Illuminationists used such terms as *ḥikmah*, *maʿrifah*, and *ʿirfān* in many cases where *metaphysics* would be used in European languages. I shall come back to this point shortly.

To return to metaphysics itself, the West of course inherited Greek philosophy, some of it directly but most of it through Arabic translations that have been made in the Islamic world. It should be remembered that it took a thousand years for the West to inherit the works of Aristotle via Arabic rather than Greek. The *Metaphysics* of Aristotle was not translated directly from Greek into Latin until after the Middle Ages. It was first translated into Arabic from Greek and Syriac, then after several centuries from Arabic into Hebrew and Latin. Moreover, since the Latin translations had commentaries by Ibn Sīnā and other major Islamic figures, in a sense, medieval Western philosophers saw the *Metaphysics* through Muslim eyes, a fact whose significance must not be overlooked. Once this work was translated, the word *metaphysics* became very important in the European Middle Ages, but before that time, for "the supreme science" Europeans had used certain other terms such as *philosophia prima* and *theosophia*, which are not in common use these days—at least not in their original meaning, especially when it comes to theosophy. For those who want to discuss metaphysics seriously, it is essential to understand such terms that were used in the West before Aristotle was widely known thanks to al-Fārābī, Ibn Sīnā, and Ibn Rushd (d. 595/1198).

Let me say a few more words about one of these terms that was used by many Christian thinkers: *theosophia*, or "theosophy" in English. This word means literally "wisdom of God," and it has an exact equivalent in Arabic: *al-ḥikmah al-ilāhiyyah*, usually translated as "Divine Wisdom." Another term that very soon became anathema in the Roman Catholic Church (although not in the Orthodox Church), because the idea that the term implied to some early Catholic thinkers was perceived as being dangerous to Catholic orthodoxy, is *gnosis*. This is a word whose authentic meaning is of critical significance for the universal understanding of metaphysics. *Gnosis* means "illuminative knowledge," "the knowledge that unifies," and "the knowledge that makes one," and of course, its root, *gn*, is in essence the same as the root *kn* found in the word *knowledge*.

One tragedy of the modern world is that the English language has a common word for the lack of gnosis, and that word is *ignorance*, but there is no clear understanding in general theological discourse for its opposite, *gnosis*, which is, therefore, far less common than the term *ignorance*. This fact is very telling of our intellectual and spiritual situation. To ignore is to disregard or negate knowing and, on the highest level, gnosis. Not only is the root *gn* in Indo-European languages related to *kn* and used in the common verb *to know* in English, but it is also reflected in the French word *connaître*, "to know," which in a sense means "to be born again." Indeed, to come to know what is essential is to be reborn. In any case, this root has to do with knowledge, but *gnosis* came to mean a very special kind of knowledge—namely, principial knowledge. It should be noted here that the word *principial* is distinct from *principle*. It is a word that a few traditionalist writers, including myself, decided to revive over half a century ago because there was no appropriate word in English corresponding to the Arabic terms *aṣīl* and *aṣālah*, which mean "principial" and "principiality." And so we began using *principial* to convey this meaning. For example, we translated *aṣālat al-wujūd* in Islamic philosophy as "principiality of existence or being."

In this sense, *gnosis* means "principial knowledge" and "knowledge that pertains to the roots of things, to their ultimate reality"; and that is none other than the heart of metaphysics as traditionally understood. In surveying the history of Western languages dealing with the subject of philosophy and even theology, one finds in them the terms *metaphysics*, *theosophy*, *gnosis*, and of course even the word *philosophy* itself. The real traditional import of all these words has to be brought out. I shall turn shortly to the relation of philosophy to the study of metaphysics.

As for the translation of *gnosis* into Islamic languages, it is usually translated as *maʿrifah* in Arabic and *ʿirfān* in Persian, Urdu, Turkish, and many other Islamic languages. In Arabic, *ʿirfān* refers to general knowledge or learning, while in Persian, it means gnosis and sapience. Sufis usually use *maʿrifah* to refer to gnosis when writing in Arabic. In other Islamic languages, especially Persian, which is the "mother" of many other Islamic languages when it comes to metaphysical discourse, however, *ʿirfān* is used for gnosis.

From the point of view of universal metaphysics, a great tragedy that occurred in the West, before even the end of the Middle Ages, was that metaphysics came to be considered as a branch of philosophy, whereas this was not the case in other traditions if one considers their whole intellectual tradition. For example, in Sufism, *ʿirfān/maʿrifah* is not a branch of philosophy, although it is such in the Peripatetic school. The writings of Ibn ʿArabī (d. 638/1240), for example, are not a branch of Islamic philosophy. Yes, they are related to philosophy, but they are not a branch of it. Although Ibn ʿArabī certainly expressed ideas that are philosophical in the most universal sense of the term, he expressed clear criticism of the "philosophers" (*falāsifah*) and distinguished his doctrine from theirs. In the Islamic tradition, the knowledge that is metaphysics retained its independence from other ways of knowing, including rational philosophy. This is as it should be, since the ultimate knowledge of metaphysics comes from the Supreme Reality, and even the means of this knowing also comes from the Supreme Reality, not from human reasoning. Both the knower and the known, the subject and the object, come from the Divine Ultimate Reality.

Now, *philosophy* as the term is usually used in the West has many different meanings, but to include metaphysics as a branch of philosophy as understood in ordinary parlance, and not *philosophia prima*, is a grave error. One could almost say that modern Western philosophy as it is taught in many universities could be better termed *misosophy*, "the hatred of wisdom," rather than *philosophy*, "the love of wisdom." Authentic metaphysics is not a branch of rational philosophy even though the term happens to have been used historically by Aristotle to describe the different parts of his philosophy: logic, natural philosophy, physics, and then metaphysics. The latter science, or *scientia sacra*, is not, however, a part of philosophy unless one is speaking about *philosophia perennis*, perennial philosophy, at the heart of which is pure metaphysics and gnosis. In the ordinary sense in which the word *philosophy* is used, metaphysics as we understand it cannot be considered as a part of it. The Islamic tradition never made the mistake of making *maʿrifah* subservient to rational philosophy, and this fact is one of the distinguishing marks of Islam. Even figures such as Ibn Sīnā, who was trying to follow the model of Aristotle, wrote some treatises that did not allow for the simple subservience of metaphysics to rational philosophy. This point cannot be overstated.

It is necessary at this juncture to turn again to certain terms drawn from Latin and sometimes from Greek and also to some Arabic words that were translated into Latin and related to what constitutes metaphysics. One of these terms, which has a medieval background, is *scientia sacra*, or "sacred science." This term was used by some Muslim authors and in the West by Saint Bonaventure, and the closely related term *scientia divina* was used by Saint Thomas Aquinas, among many others. I use *sacred science* and *scientia sacra* in two different ways: Traditional sciences that are applications of metaphysics I refer to as sacred science, whereas I refer to the metaphysical science itself—that which contains the principles of all the traditional sciences—as *scientia sacra*. In my book *Knowledge and the Sacred*, one chapter is titled "*Scientia Sacra*," and in it I summarize the principles of metaphysics.[3] I have a short synopsis there and reassert here that this is a term that has been identified

3. Seyyed Hossein Nasr, *Knowledge and the Sacred* (Albany: State University of New York Press, 1989), 130–39.

historically with supreme knowledge, and it is one that a few Western writers and I have helped resuscitate over recent decades.

Now, it is necessary to point out that in Islamic languages, in addition to the already mentioned *mā ba'd al-ṭabī'ah*, *ma'rifah*, and *'irfān* in Arabic and Persian, which are, of course, the two main languages of Islamic intellectual and spiritual discourse, there are certain other terms in Islamic languages with which metaphysics as used in its universal sense in English is equated. One of these is *al-'ilm al-a'lā*, "the supreme science," and the other is *al-ḥikmah al-ūlā*, "the prime science." These words point to a science that is at once the supreme form of knowledge and one that comes before every other science.

Next, we come to Quranic terminology for this supreme science, words that, like most other Quranic terms, have multiple levels of meaning. Those who try to limit the Quran to its external and outward meaning alone, a trend that, sadly, is becoming common in our day and age even among some Muslims, are really committing a great travesty in regard to God's Word. In contrast to this trend, we have sought to provide in *The Study Quran* various levels of meaning of different technical terms in the Sacred Book.[4] One of the basic words that is used several times in the Quran comes from the trilateral Arabic root *ḥā, kāf, mīm*, which has several meanings, including both "knowledge" and "judgment," as in the word *ḥukm*; but the meaning I want to point to is that of the Arabic word *ḥikmah*. This key term occurs in all the major Islamic languages and is not to be confused with the words *ḥukm*, *maḥkūm*, or *maḥkamah*, all of which have to do with giving legal judgment. They share the same root but have different meanings.

The basic question to ask is what the word *ḥikmah* means in the Quran when it says, "And whosoever is granted wisdom [*ḥikmah*] has been granted much good" (Q 2:269). So *ḥikmah* is a great blessing—a great good, or *khayr* in Arabic. But what does it mean? The great theologian Imām Fakhr al-Dīn al-Rāzī (d. 606/1210), who was an Ash'arite *mutakallim* opposed to *falsafah*, provides, nevertheless, an account of different meanings given to the term *ḥikmah* in Islamic thought. These meanings range from its place of greatest honor as one of the names of the Quran itself, to Islamic Law, to Islamic theology, and to Islamic philosophy and metaphysics as well as being associated with individuals who demonstrate ethical norms and correct actions. It conveys all these meanings, but it also means supreme knowledge for both Sufis and philosophers, while for Rāzī himself, it is identified with *kalām*.

4. Seyyed Hossein Nasr et al., eds., *The Study Quran: A New Translation and Commentary* (New York: HarperOne, 2015). All translations from the Quran in this book have been taken from *The Study Quran*.

Throughout Islamic civilization, this word has always carried an aura of great honor, prestige, and appreciation. In this sense, a person who has attained a very high level of realization is called a *ḥakīm* (pl. *ḥukamāʾ*), a word that has two meanings in everyday discourse in Islamic civilization. It refers to a person who is a physician and also to one who is wise and, more specifically, a traditional philosopher and metaphysician. This dual meaning also reflects the close relationship between medicine and philosophy in Islam. In fact, the most celebrated Islamic physician, Ibn Sīnā, was also the most famous philosopher.

Ibn Sīnā, Ibn Rushd, and many other earlier Islamic philosophers were also physicians, although the later ones tended to make their living from the practice and teaching of Islamic Law rather than medicine. Usually, *ḥikmah*—that is, traditional philosophy and especially metaphysics, which lies at its heart—was considered so precious intellectually and spiritually that it would never be taught for monetary remuneration. Rather, this profound wisdom was passed on freely to qualified and dedicated seekers of truth. This assertion should not be seen as contradicting what we said above about metaphysics not being a branch of philosophy. In that assertion, we had the general sense of philosophy in mind, whereas by traditional Islamic philosophy, we mean the *ḥikmah* tradition, in which metaphysics is not a branch but its heart, origin, and end.

On a personal note, it was my great fortune to be able to study with some of the foremost masters of the science of *ḥikmah* in Iran. These remarkable teachers never accepted any form of payment, not even a small gift such as a book. It was a *sunnah* not to accept payment for teaching *ḥikmah*, and that is why traditional philosophers made their living through *fiqh* (jurisprudence) or medicine and why, from the early centuries of Islam, the word *ḥakīm* came to have these two meanings of "physician" and "metaphysician" that persist to our own day in Arabic, Persian, Turkish, Urdu, and other Islamic languages.

As for the word *ḥakīm*, which comes from the Quranic term *ḥikmah*, it is understood in Sufism and the *ḥikmah* tradition to refer to a person with knowledge of the supreme *sophia*, or supreme wisdom, and therefore metaphysics or *philosophia prima*. Sufi treatises employed this word, and in fact, Ibn ʿArabī writes in *al-Futūḥāt al-makkiyyah* that the word *ḥikmah* refers to the highest wisdom—that is, knowledge concerning the Nature of God, our relation to that Nature, and the means to attain the knowledge thereof.

So in one way or another, there are multiple meanings associated with *ḥikmah*, none identical to the other but each representing a rich field of meaning when it comes to the discussion of knowledge in general and metaphysics in particular. Furthermore, to understand them is to become cognizant of the very rich and diverse intellectual field with which Islamic metaphysicians, philosophers, and Sufis were deeply concerned. Involvement in these matters was not restricted to only one school of thought or to a particular region; rather, it was prevalent throughout the Islamic world. During the many centuries of Islamic history, there have been *ḥukamāʾ* throughout the Indian subcontinent, the Malay world, Black Africa, and the Ottoman and, of course, the Persian and Arab worlds.

A *ḥakīm* is a person who knows the truth in a principial way, who knows what truly is worth knowing. The closest translation into English of the word *ḥakīm* would be "sage," although this is a word not used often anymore. Fifty-some years ago, I titled my book of lectures at Harvard *Three Muslim Sages* despite requests to use the word *philosophers* instead.[5] I used the term *sage* because it carries a meaning beyond the word *philosopher* in the present-day Anglo-Saxon world, especially with the limitations of philosophy since the nineteenth century with the coming of logical positivism, analytical philosophy, and so forth, which I described earlier as "misosophy" rather than philosophy because they have no interest in true wisdom and in fact negate the significance of *sophia*. A sage, however, is always concerned with wisdom. In earlier eras in Western society, there were people who were called sages, but unfortunately, they have all but disappeared. In the West, it is exceedingly rare to find someone at whose feet one can sit, as one still does in certain parts of the Islamic world or India, and learn wisdom from him or her. That is one of the great tragedies of the current age.

It is now necessary to turn to another issue, which has to do with where we can find real metaphysics today. As we look at various civilizations, this question remains pertinent. In almost every traditional civilization this kind of knowledge was hidden from the eye of the general public. It was reserved for the few. Now, to criticize this situation as elitist in a pejorative sense is a result of ignorance of what is involved and is not even logical. Graduate classes in mathematics or physics, for example, are open only to those who have spent years acquiring the prerequisite knowledge to be able to follow the classes and benefit from them. No one accuses anyone involved in these classes, neither teachers nor students, of being elitist, but when it comes to esoterism and metaphysics, the same principle of restricted access to its study is often criticized. Furthermore, those who do the accusing are assuming that the term *elitist* has a pejorative meaning.

5. Seyyed Hossein Nasr, *Three Muslim Sages* (Cambridge, MA: Harvard University Press, 1964).

Elite in the real sense, however, reflects the reality that different people excel in different fields and are gifted in particular domains. One person may be an excellent sitar player but not know integral calculus; another person may be good at quantum mechanics but not have any inclination for or knowledge of moral philosophy. In modern Western civilization, fields such as architecture or physics or mathematics are left to specialists, but when it comes to discussions of theology, metaphysics, and religion in general, many people consider their views to be of equal significance in comparison to the views of those who have acquired profound knowledge in these matters through years of study. The suggestion to such people that they need to learn more is taken by them as an affront, but if a professor tells a freshman student, "Albert Einstein's theory of relativity is not for you now; wait until you have studied classical physics for a few more years and then see if you have the capability to study relativity," the student would not be offended. So yes, in the same manner, a restriction on the teaching of metaphysics is elitist in the sense that it requires both the proper training and the special gift, for all people have not been created by God to be metaphysicians.

For those who do have this calling and capability to acquire sapience, where do they go to pursue it? The person who seeks after this kind of knowledge is one who is not fully satisfied with only the mundane externalities of life—a family, a career, material comforts, or even social activism, which to a certain extent can take one beyond oneself. The person qualified to study serious metaphysics is one who feels that his or her very reason for living is to pursue answers to ultimate, fundamental, existential questions and is capable of finding authentic answers to questions such as, Why are we here? Where did we come from? Where are we going and where should we be going? What happens to us after death? Now, to where will this person turn for answers? In all traditions—Islamic, Hindu, Christian, Buddhist, Jewish, and others—the discipline that addressed these questions was not offered in the marketplace of ideas to just anyone; a person had to truly seek it, be capable of understanding it, and be willing to sacrifice everything in order to attain it. Why did Christ say "Seek, and ye shall find" (Matthew 7:7)? Why does one have to seek? Should it not be available to everyone? The fact that it must be sought implies that not everyone can find and understand it and that not everyone is a seeker. The very fact that Christ says "Seek, and ye shall find" means that there is something one can find only by seeking. And regarding this issue, there is an even more direct saying of Christ: "Many are called, but few are chosen" (Matthew 22:14). Many modern Christians who consider Christ as a "prophet of democracy," as having loved everyone equally, cannot find a way to defend this saying and thus prefer to ignore it. Is God unfair? No. Some people have certain callings, and Christianity is full of references to those truths, although they are often overlooked these days.

In the traditions that are still very much alive and have preserved their inner dimensions, which is where the teachings of metaphysics are to be found, there are some important concepts related to this dimension to which we need to turn again. First of all, let us look at the adjective *esoteric*, which in common parlance simply refers to something that is rare, hidden, or hard to understand. It is used to describe even the rules of some games and sports that are played rarely. This is not, however, the meaning of this key word in my writings or in traditional writings in general. *Eso* in Greek means "in"; *esoteric* means "that which is inward," "that which is inside." In looking at other people, we observe their outward aspect. When they speak, something of their inwardness comes out, but we still do not fully know their inwardness, obviously, and they do not know ours. We have an inner world within us, and God Himself describes Himself as having an inward dimension: *Huwa'l-Awwalu wa'l-Ākhiru wa'l-Ẓāhiru wa'l-Bāṭinu* (Q 57:3; He is the First, and the Last, and the Outward, and the Inward). God is, therefore, also the Inward; inwardness is a Divine Quality. Every outwardness has an inwardness; everything outward has an inner aspect. The often-used word *phenomenon* comes from the Greek *phainomenon*, meaning "that which appears." But from where does the appearance come? It arises from the inward. The very word *phenomenon* implies an inner essence, or *noumenon*. And the word *appearance* in English always implies a subject of which the appearance is the appearance. There is no phenomenon without noumenon, contrary to the modern scientific claim, a science that is by its own definition concerned only with phenomena.

In Islam we have the term *ʿilm al-bāṭin*, the science of the inward associated especially with Sufism. This word is not to be confused, however, with the label *bāṭiniyyah*, which was sometimes applied to the Ismailis, especially in the eleventh and twelfth centuries. That appellation represents a complex set of issues in the history of Islamic thought into which I will not go here. *Ahl al-bāṭin*, meaning "people associated with the inner path" or "people associated with spiritual reality," is used to this very day for certain sages. This was, for example, the title of one of the greatest gnostics and Sufis of Persian in the nineteenth century, Āqā Muḥammad Riḍā Qumshaʾī (d. 1306/1888). He was one of the foremost saints and traditional philosophers, an incredible sage who wrote poems, taught and commented on Ibn ʿArabī and Mullā Ṣadrā (d. 1050/1640), and was said to have performed *karāmāt*, or "miracles."

Having discussed the word *bāṭin*, let us now turn to the word *ʿilm* itself, which has become secularized to a large extent even in modern Arabic and other Islamic languages. Students of physics might say that they are learning *'ilm al-fizīqah* in Arabic. Traditionally, however, *'Alīm* is a Quality of God: *Huwa'l-'Alīm*, "He is the Knower [*al-'Alīm*], the Wise [*al-Ḥakīm*]" (Q 12:83, 12:100, 66:2). It is interesting to note here that the term *'ārif* is not a Divine Name—that is, the principial knowledge denoted by the word *'ārif* is not linguistically associated with a Name of God—whereas *al-'Alīm is* a Name of God. This difference demonstrates, as Ibn 'Arabī has said, that in a sense, *'ilm* at its highest level stands even above *ma'rifah. 'Ilm*, the real *'ilm*, is supreme metaphysics, supreme knowledge, *scientia sacra*, because the knowledge that God has of Himself by nature of being *al-'Alīm* is knowledge of Reality without any veils; it is that knowledge that is the ultimate source of all knowledge. Moreover, *'ilm* means both "knowledge *by* God" and "knowledge *of* God."

All authentic knowledge that we have is essentially related to Divine Knowledge. This is, in fact, the central subject of my book *Knowledge and the Sacred*. Real knowledge itself, even knowledge of everyday matters, implies the light of God's Knowledge. If God were not *al-'Alīm*, we would not even know the time of day or other such mundane facts. All human knowledge is a reflection of God's Knowledge of Himself and of His creation, and it is only by virtue of the knowledge He has placed in us that our knowledge of Him can come about. In the same way that no one can love God without God loving him or her, so too no one can know God without God knowing that person and allowing him or her to know Him.

Of course, although God knows us in principle, He does not *have to* "remember" us; God can also "forget" us if we forget Him. This is mentioned in the Quran: "They forgot God; so He forgot them" (Q 9:67). In principle, this does not mean that Divine Knowledge considered in the metaphysical and theological sense is limited, because Divine Knowledge is infinite. Having God's direct Knowledge of us, having His attention bestowed upon us, is that which makes it possible for us to know God. When a person forgets God, it is because God has already "forgotten" that person because of the state of spiritual negligence into which he or she has fallen. Metaphysically speaking, every act issues from the cause to the effect, not from the effect to the cause. Everything originates from the Divine Principle even though we see only our part of the act and our reactions to it.

The next question that should come up, now that we understand something of the word *metaphysics* and its cognate terms dealing with principial knowledge and we perceive that knowledge that illuminates and transforms and unites us with that which is the Principle of all beings—with God Himself in the theological language of the Abrahamic families—is the following: With what does this supreme science deal? With what does metaphysics deal? Now, again, this brings us to a very complex set of problems that I shall touch on here. In the Western tradition, some might look back to Aristotle. In the book *Lambda* of his *Metaphysica*, he says that the subject of metaphysics is being qua being, or *ōn* in Greek. He goes on to say that this highest science is the science of Being, or what we now call theologically God as pure Being. The highest level of authentic metaphysics, however, reaches even beyond the level of the Unmoved Mover mentioned by Aristotle. That Reality is the ultimate goal of universal metaphysics, the Reality that is even beyond Being. It is the Beyond-Being or Non-Being, the Supreme Tao mentioned at the beginning of the *Tao Te Ching*. It is the inconceivable Reality to which our mind can point but cannot encompass. As the Persian poet Saʿdī (d. 691/1292) says,

ای برتر از خیال و قیاس و گمان و وهم
وز هر چه گفته اند و شنیدیم و خوانده ایم

O Thou Who art beyond imagination, analogy, opinion, and fantasy,
And beyond everything that they have said and that we have heard and read.[6]

It is remarkable that for nearly every metaphysical principle, there is a Persian poem that pertains to it, provided that one knows how to interpret the poem, and one might add that the same is true of Arabic.

The Divine Principle is beyond everything, including Pure Being, whose concept is the most universal idea that our minds can hold. Not only is the Divine Principle beyond Being; it is not even limited by the condition of being beyond Being. Clearly this is a difficult concept to understand. In classical Islamic metaphysics, the Divine Essence is called *al-dhāt bi-lā ism wa bi-lā rasm* in Arabic—that is, the Divine Essence that is beyond name and definition. This Reality first takes us to the concept of *wujūd*, provided that no conditions are set upon it (*lā bi-sharṭ*); then to the condition of negation of all otherness upon it (*bi-sharṭ lā*); and then to the condition of "something" set upon it (*bi-sharṭ al-shayʾ*). Finally, we come to the highest Reality, which is completely unconditioned. This Reality is completely above all others, and yet It Itself is the ground for the divisions we have made thus far without having any condition imposed upon It (*lā bi-sharṭ maqsamī*). It is difficult to understand It by means of logical categories alone. The whole doctrine leads to pure transcendence and, at the same time, immanence.

6. Saʿdī, *Gulistān*, ed. Muḥammad Jawād Mashkūr (Tehran: Iqbāl, 1963), 3.

When we reach pure transcendence and pure immanence, metaphysics in human language stops.[7] Yet, although this is a science that is difficult to expound fully in writing or to teach in a class, it is not impossible to do so even under modern conditions. Matters were easier in traditional settings. Students of traditional metaphysics in Persia had the opportunity to sit at the feet of the greatest masters of gnosis and metaphysics and learn directly through traditional texts basic ideas that became instilled in their hearts and minds. These masters also benefited students through their spiritual presence, which is usually associated with oral transmission. To some extent, the same was done for students of traditional sciences in general, but this method was particularly appropriate for teaching metaphysics, which is abstruse and difficult for most seekers to grasp fully. When teaching this supreme science, traditionally masters chose their students carefully and combined the written with the oral, at times even teaching through silence. The serious study of metaphysics is in fact a study of the Real as such, a subject that is ultimately beyond every conception, every determination, and every limit. Furthermore, it is even beyond the concept of being, beyond every definition and every determination, that latter proviso being itself a condition. To understand this doctrine, one must deal with that which is boundless and limitless, beyond all determination and definition. In addition, it must be remembered that this understanding requires serious spiritual and intellectual preparation, contemplation and meditation, illumination, and also grace from the Divine.

Many metaphysical texts begin with That which is absolute and infinite, boundless and without limit. One of the most beautiful expressions of this truth is found at the beginning of the *Tao Te Ching*, one of the world's most important sacred scriptures: "The way of which one can speak as 'way' is

7. As a complement to what we have said, it is helpful here to include Lord Northbourne's relevant definition of metaphysics (or what he calls "metaphysic"):

> The word "metaphysical" comes from the Greek. It does not mean "beyond the physical" in the current sense of the last word, but rather "beyond the natural," that is to say "beyond the observable." It is therefore equivalent to the Latin "supernatural," provided that the latter is understood literally and not in its degraded sense, in which it is applied to almost any unexplained phenomenon. Properly speaking, neither word is concerned with phenomena as such, but exclusively with the universal principles underlying all phenomena, explicable or otherwise; and that is as much as to say—with the "mystery" in the ancient sense (from a Greek word meaning "to be silent"). Therefore the language of metaphysic is always symbolical and not descriptive; it must leave room for the inexpressible. (Lord Northbourne, "Religion and Science," in *Science and the Myth of Progress*, ed. Mehrdad M. Zarandi [Bloomington, IN: World Wisdom, 2003], 90n12)

not the eternal Way (Tao)."[8] This verse corresponds to the Islamic *lā ilāha illā'Llāh* (There is no god but God). The name for the Divine Principle that can be named is not *the* Name or Reality of that Principle. To name something is to limit it. No matter what is said about the Real, It is beyond that appellation and description. Pure metaphysics begins with that Absolute Reality that is paradoxically beyond even the concept of absoluteness, because It in a sense also includes the nonabsolute, the relative, and is beyond our ordinary human mental capacity to comprehend and encompass, no matter how intelligent we are. The extent to which we can comprehend it is granted to us by the Transcendent Itself. Some people are made for this kind of intellection and understanding; some are not.

Then we have the self-determination of Absolute Reality that determines and discloses Itself, there being nothing outside of It to do such a thing. It determines Itself, and Its first autodetermination is Being, or *Esse* in Latin. Now, this is where all Western metaphysics really begins. Saints Thomas Aquinas and Bonaventure, among the greatest metaphysicians of the Middle Ages, begin with pure *Esse*, pure Being, and many Islamic philosophers begin there also. The great Persian philosopher Mullā Ṣadrā says in book 1 of his *Asfār* and elsewhere that God is pure Being and is not bound by any determination or condition. This opens the door to the concept of Beyond Being that is alluded to directly in the *Tao Te Ching* and is also mentioned in Ismaili texts. We find it in the Upanishads as well when Yājñavalkya asks the master, "What is Brahman?" to which the master replies, "Neti, neti" (Neither this nor that). No matter how Yājñavalkya tries to define it, he is told, "Neti, neti." It is beyond everything we can conceive, everything we can say. God is beyond everything we can imagine, and yet He is also the source of everything we can conceive. He is the source of everything that exists, and so His first self-determination is Being.

Now, it is this cardinal doctrine that has been denied by mainstream modern European philosophy. Leibniz (d. 1716) was perhaps the last person among the well-known Western philosophers to address it seriously, along with Malebranche (d. 1715), who was a student of Descartes (d. 1650). Since the seventeenth century, Western philosophy has not been concerned much with ontology, not to speak of the Beyond-Being, with just a few peripheral exceptions. Those seeking an authentic understanding of traditional doctrines concerning Non-Being and Being should not be misled by what Martin Heidegger (d. 1976) says about *Sein* and *Dasein*. Heidegger was, of course, a very

8. Seyyed Hossein Nasr, *A Sufi Commentary on the Tao Te Ching: The Way and Its Virtue*, trans. Mohammad H. Faghfoory (Louisville: Fons Vitae, 2025), 27.

important German philosopher whose significance I do not want to belittle, but his writings have misled many people in search of traditional ontology. Most people believe he revived the study of being and existence in the West, but what he refers to as *Existenz* concerns primarily human existence and life. It is important to remember that his understanding of *Sein* is not Being as Mullā Ṣadrā or Sabzawārī (d. 1289/1873) or even Ibn Sīnā understood it.

Henry Corbin (d. 1978), my dear friend and colleague for many years in Iran and France, met with Heidegger in Freiburg in Germany when Corbin was young, and he later translated Heidegger's *Was ist Metaphysik?* into French. It was the first work of Heidegger to be translated into French, and it was instrumental in the rise of modern French existentialism with Jean-Paul Sartre (d. 1980), Simone de Beauvoir (d. 1986), and others. Corbin once said to me that for Heidegger, existence leads to death, whereas for Mullā Ṣadrā, it leads to eternal life; that is, it is being that opens up unto the eternal. So it would be a mistake to think that Heidegger's discussion of *Sein*, which in German means "being," and *Dasein*, which means broadly "existence," is the same thing as *wujūd*. And so students of metaphysics should not be misled by the books, written sometimes even by Muslims, that compare Heidegger's "ontology" to the Islamic philosophical concept of *wujūd*. These are not at all similar.

The writers who really opened the door to the highest understanding of *wujūd* in the traditional sense were Guénon and Frithjof Schuon (d. 1998). It was their expositions that opened the door to the full understanding of the metaphysics of Being and also Non-Being or Beyond-Being. For its part, academic philosophy in the West either denies the reality of this category completely—as seen in the works of many analytic philosophers who deny the significance, relevance, and even reality of being as such—or speaks of it in terms of agnostic existentialism and even *angst*, but these views do not and cannot really define being in the metaphysical sense. Authentic metaphysics deals first of all with Beyond-Being, and after that with Being, then Existence, followed by existence.

Metaphysics deals most of all with Supreme Reality and also with the grades of reality that issue from It, but it does so in relation to that Supreme Reality and not as independent realms. Following traditional writings, I have spent many years trying to clarify the usage of terms associated with this supreme science because there is so much confusion in modern philosophical discourse around them. Classical philosophy was like today's chemistry in that each word was clearly defined, whereas in much of modern European philosophy, there is a great deal of ambiguity in the terminology that is used. This ambiguity is the reason that those in the field of analytical philosophy are always trying to clarify terms, even though they often disregard some of the most important meanings and also neglect symbolism and the hierarchic levels of meaning of many words. Take *existence*, for example. Of course, this word can refer to the existence of a material object such as a tree, a car, and so on. An object that is defined as having existence (with a lowercase *e*) possesses some form of reality, and its everyday meaning seems clear enough, although its philosophical meaning, relation to quiddity, and many other philosophical issues are not so obvious and need authentic philosophical insight to understand, not to speak of such terms as *existentialism* that are derived from it. When we discuss Existence (with a capital *E*), we are referring to the act of Being (with a capital *B*) that existentiates the cosmos. The Quran says of God, "His Command when He desires a thing is only to say to it, 'Be!' and it is [*kun fa-yakūn*]" (Q 36:82). *Kun* concerns the command form of the verb *kāna*, and *kawn*, from the same root, means "the cosmos" or "the world" in Arabic and is related to the Aramaic and Syriac word *knono*. Now, that command of God, *kun*, is not God Himself; God is the One Who issues the command *kun*; so obviously, *kun* is not God—*kun* concerns the realm of existence. This scriptural passage should make this concept in its relation to God easier to understand. And then, of course, there is the question of the world in relation to the Divine Principle and its creative power, an issue to which I shall turn in the next two lectures.

Another function of metaphysics is that it provides an understanding of the fundamental Attributes and Characteristics of the Real. The Real is beyond all attributes, and at the same time, It is the source of all positive attributes. Consider how not only true but also beautiful *lā ilāha illā'Llāh* is. It is the perfect expression of pure metaphysics on the highest level. There is no reality except the Absolute Reality, and then from that Reality (the *illā*) issues *Muḥammadun rasūl Allāh*, "Muhammad is the messenger of God," whose metaphysical meaning is that every positive manifestation comes from God, for the Prophet in his inner reality is not only a man in the ordinary sense, although he is so outwardly; he also represents the perfection of God's creation and contains in his inner reality as *al-Ḥaqīqah al-muḥammadiyyah*, or the Muḥammadan Reality, all positive cosmic qualities. Thus we see that all positive qualities are, in a sense, *rusul*, or "messengers," sent by God. In the esoteric dimension of Islam, these two fundamental *shahādatayn*, declarations or testimonies of faith, *lā ilāha illā'Llāh* and *Muḥammadun rasūl Allāh*, contain the metaphysical and cosmological teachings that show that the Source is beyond all things; yet all that is positive flows from that Source. Ultimately, the principles of religion are contained in the *shahādatayn*. Moreover, the Blessed Prophet is the best and most beautiful of God's creation (*aḥsan*). He is the supreme *namūdhaj*—that is, "exemplification"—as well as the immediate principle of all the positive qualities manifested in the cosmos and in man.

To rephrase this doctrine, the *shahādatayn* correspond to two aspects of metaphysical truth. First of all, the two testimonies of faith enable us to understand the Real to the extent possible by removing all mental confines or limitations that our minds may put upon It, thus opening our consciousnesses toward the Illimitable and the Infinite. Secondly, they show us that all that is positive comes from that Absolute and Infinite Reality that we cannot comprehend in the ordinary sense of the word because *to comprehend* means "to embrace" or "to enfold" (*comprehendere* in Latin means "to put one's arms around something"), and God is Infinite; therefore, we cannot "put our arms around" Him. We cannot comprehend Him as we do other realities. We can only immerse ourselves in the ocean of His Infinite Reality.

All authentic metaphysics deals with the Divine Principle or God as the Absolute, the Infinite, and pure Goodness. These are the three fundamental Qualities of God from which, in a sense, flow all the Divine Names—all the ninety-nine Most Beautiful Names of Allah, *al-asmā' al-ḥusnā*, revealed in Islam—which are among the greatest spiritual gifts of Islam to all humanity. No other religion has so many sanctified Names of God revealed in it. There are a dozen or so Divine Names in Christianity, a few in Buddhism in its own nontheistic way, a few in Hinduism. One could say that the ninety-nine Names of God in Islam were revealed because it was the terminal religion for this world, the *khatm*, or "seal," of revelation, and so these many Names of Himself that God revealed in Islam are, in a sense, all different doors that open through His Mercy unto His ineffable Essence. Each Divine Name is a door to *Allāh ta'ālā* both in Its ordinary meaning and in that it provides the possibility of the act of walking through It to the One.

"Absoluteness of the One" is the ultimate meaning of *lā ilāha illā'Llāh*, which in the deepest sense means that there is no reality but Allah, the Real. The character of Ultimate Reality belongs to Him alone; there is no second to Him as the source of existence. Absoluteness denies all secondary reality, all relativity, all otherness. To be two is to be in the realm of the relative; it is to enter into relationality—relationality and relativity are related etymologically, obviously. So *lā ilāha illā'Llāh* means being One in the absolute sense, with no otherness being comparable to It, and in the deeper sense, with no otherness even having any existence. Or one could say with the Sufis, *lā wujūda wa lā mawjūda illā'Llāh* (There is no existence and no existent but God).

Now, the other quintessential aspect of the Divine Reality is Infinitude, which is all-inclusive as absoluteness is all-exclusive. The Quran refers often to this aspect of Reality in pointing out that all comes from Him—for example, when it states, *Bi-yadihi malakūtu kulli shay'in* (Q 36:83; In Whose Hand lies the dominion [spiritual root] of all things). Nothing can exist in any domain of manifestation that does not have its roots in God. Moreover, God's creation as a whole is indefinite, reflecting His Infinitude. Creation is unlimited, indeterminate in its possibilities, unbounded. We cannot bind it or set a limit to it. In a sense, it is like the classical mathematical infinite series xn, where *n* goes from 1 to infinity; even the integers 1, 2, 3, 4, 5, and so on have no end. No matter how much one counts, the numbers could still go on; logically, there is no end to them. This is, in fact, a mathematical reflection of metaphysical infinitude, the Divine Infinitude. There are many subtle aspects to this doctrine, including the aspect of the reflection of the Divine Absoluteness present in the male nature and of the Divine Infinitude in the female nature. The Quran alludes to this matter, as do certain *aḥādīth*. These are very subtle issues that have various applications in many domains into which I shall not go here.

Now let us turn to Divine Goodness, with which metaphysics is also concerned. Not only is God Infinite and Absolute; He is also Goodness and the Source of all that can be considered to be good and beautiful. Again, there is a set of Divine Qualities such as *Raḥmah* (Mercy), *Karāmah* (Generosity), *Jamāl* (Beauty), *Maghfirah* (Forgiveness), and others that deal with Divine Goodness in one way or another and that issue from the Divine Nature. One of the functions of metaphysics is the study of the root meaning of these Qualities. In Islam, many theologians and Sufis, including luminaries such as Fakhr al-Dīn al-Rāzī, al-Ghazzālī, and Ibn ʿArabī, have written works on the Divine Names. In fact, it is a favorite subject among many Islamic sages, the reason being that these Names are keys to the understanding of the Divine Nature and the path of human perfection in the spiritual and metaphysical sense as well as keys to the understanding of cosmology. Their meaning can be understood on different levels, from the linguistic to the theological and from the metaphysical to the cosmological, but the highest level, of course, is the metaphysical, in which they are revealed as actual windows allowing the vision and perception of the Divine Nature. The fact that God revealed Himself in this manner in Islam is something quite remarkable. I do not say this as an exclusivist or chauvinist when it comes to Islam. I am a defender of all the religions that God has sent, and I believe that all heavenly revealed religions provide such windows and should be respected as the Quran itself respects them, as seen in many verses where it refers to *al-dīn* (religion) in the universal sense.

It is certainly worth considering just how much and how fully God has revealed Himself through His Names in the Quranic revelation and how rare this is in the realm of religion considered in general. We do not know all the religions that have existed throughout human history. Perhaps God revealed other truths in other ages; we do not know. But we do know that in every religion, God reveals some aspect of Himself, and it is metaphysics that is able to understand the universal and inner meaning of these revelations. What does it mean when we say God is *Karīm* (Generous); what is the full meaning of *Karīm*? These are Names that are completely inward in their deepest meaning. God is *Jamīl* (Beautiful). But what is Divine Beauty? Where do we find answers to these questions?

In the Islamic tradition, answers to such questions can be found primarily in the treatises on gnosis and metaphysics written usually by Sufis or *ḥakīms*. It is often asked why traditional Islamic thought did not develop aesthetics as a separate intellectual discipline as we see in Western Christianity. The question is, in a sense, absurd, since Islam did create one of the most beautiful civilizations of the world, and there must therefore have existed a distinct Islamic aesthetic. It is a question that is asked in the West, however, because while one can buy books on logic, ethics, and aesthetics belonging to the tradition of Western thought, in Islam, a discussion of aesthetics is usually found as a part of a chapter in a treatise on Sufism or general philosophy; there is not a single book of philosophy devoted solely to aesthetics in its current connotation in Arabic or Persian before modern times. The answer to this question lies in the fact that the questioner is looking in the wrong place. A discussion of aesthetics is to be found primarily in the writings of the Sufis. The *Mathnawī* of Jalāl al-Dīn Rūmī (d. 672/1273), for example, is one of the most profound books of aesthetics ever written, but as of now, scholars have not bothered to pull out all the verses concerned with aesthetics in the contemporary sense, systematize them, and present them as such.

The Divine Qualities and Names related to beauty, *Jamīl* and *Jamāl*, deal with the very Essence of God as well as with His theophanies. That is why beauty pulls us to the very center of our being; it melts us. There is no possibility of spiritual realization without *iḥsān* and beauty. Moreover, while one of the meanings of *ḥusn* is "beauty," the other is "virtue." That is why beauty is so powerful as a means of interiorizing the soul and why, in a certain sense, Islam is based more on beauty than even on love understood humanly. Christianity, however, is based more on love than on beauty—without, of course, neglecting the latter—and so, as a result of the weakening of traditional Christianity today, many modern Christians do not care much whether a church looks beautiful or ugly. Some modern churches look more like office buildings than houses of God. They are far away from such Christian architectural masterpieces as the cathedrals of Chartres or Notre Dame.

Unfortunately, some Muslims are emulating this trend toward decadent religious architecture in the West by building ugly mosques, some of which look like warehouses. This is in stark contrast to classical Islamic civilization, where architects and artisans and even ordinary people sought to create beauty in all that they made. Objects that were made in the Islamic world for practical everyday use—even a cloth used as a towel just a century ago in a public bath—are now viewed as works of art and are displayed in museums or framed in people's homes because they were made so beautifully.

So we see that in traditional Islamic civilization, beauty was everywhere, but who could explain the deeper meaning of this beauty? The explanation was found in Islamic metaphysics and especially among the Sufis in the works of masters such as Awḥad-al-Dīn Kirmānī (d. 635/1238) and Jalāl al-Dīn Rūmī, who could be called the supreme troubadour of beauty. There are many others as well. To make their works available for the world today is a very important undertaking for the present-day generation. Beauty is a major gateway to metaphysics and gnosis.

The role of metaphysics is also to make possible the understanding of the relative in light of the Absolute, and so it provides the basis and the key for sciences that are concerned with not only the relative as relative (as is modern science) but also the relative in light of the Divine, of the Absolute—and that understanding is what Islam requires for every form of authentic knowledge. In the traditional universe, every form of real knowledge is related ultimately to God. The whole intellectual heritage of Islam is based on this truth, from *fiqh* to poetry to philosophy to cosmology and everything in between.

Furthermore, it is the role of metaphysics to provide the principles of all knowledge, and here Aristotle was right; the root of all forms of real knowledge, of all sciences, is to be found in metaphysics, and Islamic civilization put this truth into effect. For example, in the field of Islamic medicine, Ibn Sīnā was one of the first to discuss the philosophical basis of the human body using metaphysical ideas. In the field of mathematics, ʿUmar Khayyām (d. ca. 523/1129) begins his *On Proofs for Problems Concerning Algebra* with a metaphysical introduction to the roots of mathematics as being in the Divine Mind or Intellect in the principial sense. The same can be found in other fields, including even *fiqh* or *kalām*. Even in the sciences in today's world, although metaphysics is forgotten, it is still in authentic sciences that one must seek the principles of traditional cosmology, physics, and anthropology, and it is there that one finds the key that provides the understanding of symbolism in the traditional arts, both music and poetry, as well as the plastic arts.

And finally, it is metaphysics that produces the most important support for the understanding of what the basis of ethics individually and in the social order is and should be: What is good and why should we be good? Many people are motivated to be good because their parents or some elder has said they should be good and that is enough for them, but for others, that is not enough, and every civilization must have an answer for those others who seek solutions to questions like these. Otherwise, that young man or woman who is asking such things will go elsewhere outside religion and tradition, and the unity of the social order will become thereby endangered. The role of metaphysics in providing responses that are comprehensible to intelligent seekers when it comes to questions of ethics and social structures must not be forgotten and lost in all the contemporary research that is going on in these domains today.

I shall end this lecture with just one question: Today, where does one find such metaphysical teachings? Where do we find this knowledge? The simple answer is that only the heart of traditional religion can provide it. No ordinary philosopher in the philosophy department of Oxford or Harvard universities can provide it. I am not speaking here of one particular religion; I am speaking of religion as such—its inner, esoteric heart, so difficult to obtain these days but not impossible. According to the *ḥadīth* of the Prophet, *lā takhlū'l-arḍ ʿan ḥujjati'Llāh* (The earth shall never be empty of the proof of God). There are those whose very presence is a proof of the reality and presence of God, and we are all invited to join them. This is the meaning of the saying of Christ: *ʿalayhi'l-salām* (Seek, and ye shall find). All such teachings refer to the necessity of a kind of *anamnesis*—that is, a recollection in the Platonic sense of remembering, of waking up. Once we wake up, we realize that the pure knowledge we have been seeking is standing right in front of us and within us. But we must seek it, and if we do so earnestly and are qualified by the Grace of God, we shall find the spring of principial knowledge, of authentic metaphysics, and be able to drink from it.

QUESTIONS AND ANSWERS

Hamza Yusuf: *Bismi'Llāh.* First of all, thank you so much for coming. We are all honored to have you here. I do not know if everybody here realizes the high regard in which you are held in the non-Muslim community in the West as one of today's living philosophers.

Seyyed Hossein Nasr: *Astaghfiru'Llāh.*

HY: So, may Allah reward you. I have several questions, but I am going to limit them to two. First, you mentioned Malebranche; is there any evidence that he got his occasionalism from the Islamic tradition?

SHN: The Lebanese professor Majid Fakhry (d. 2021), among others, has argued that the occasionalism of Malebranche comes from Ashʿarism, and I believe that there is something to that assertion. Although we have no hard proof to back up this claim, we can point to the writings of David Hume (d. 1776) in which he posits that causality can be negated, and he provides examples. I might give the example of a person putting a knife on cheese and cutting it and then ask, "Does the knife cut the cheese or does God will the knife to go into the cheese?" Now, of all the millions of examples that could be given, David Hume gave an example that is also found in the writings of al-Ghazzālī: that of a piece of cotton being burnt by fire. Logically, we could infer from this fact that Hume had read al-Ghazzālī's view in some text, even in the eighteenth century. So surely Malebranche, who lived 150 years before David Hume, could also have been influenced by it. Majid Fakhry, who knew medieval Western philosophy well, discussed this matter in his famous book published in 1958, *Islamic Occasionalism*.[9] He alludes in this work to the example of David Hume as possible evidence for the Islamic tradition being the source of Malebranche's occasionalism, and I, as a humble scholar of Islamic philosophy, do not want to give an ex cathedra statement saying, "Definitely, yes." But I am on the side of those who believe it very likely that Malebranche picked up this idea, originally from Islamic sources, that was being discussed in Catholic circles in the sixteenth and seventeenth centuries. Although Descartes had criticized scholastic philosophy, it was still being taught in almost all Catholic seminaries at the time. Thus I am sure that the ideas of al-Ashʿarī (d. 324/936) and al-Ghazzālī were still being taught in some places where Malebranche studied.

HY: Thank you. The second question I have is about the Arabic term *wujūd* and finding the right word to translate it into English. Some translators in the books of *kalām* use "existence," but obviously there are problems with that word.

SHN: In fact, I have written an essay on the subject of how to translate the Arabic term *wujūd*, and I have mentioned that it can be translated

9. Majid Fakhry, *Islamic Occasionalism and Its Critique by Averroës and Aquinas* (New York: Routledge, 2008).

into four different English words, depending on the situation in which the word *wujūd* is being used in Arabic.[10] It can mean "Being" with a capital *B*. It can mean "being" with a small *b* (embracing the use of the term *mawjūdāt*, or "beings" or "existents"). *Wujūd* can also mean "Existence" with a capital *E* in the sense that I mentioned earlier using the Quranic quote *kun fa-yakūn*, referring to the existentiating aspect of Pure Being. And it could be translated as "existence" with a small *e*, meaning the *wujūd*, or existence, of objects such as the table in the corner.

Questioner 1: My question has to do with the relationship between metaphysics and epistemology. When Western philosophers try to expound metaphysics, the problem they are concerned with is how to show these metaphysical contents epistemically. How does this relate to Islamic metaphysics, and how does one show these epistemically? In the case of Heidegger, he chooses to discuss being in terms of the human being, in terms of epistemology, in terms of connecting the human being to what he knows. How would one do that in Islamic metaphysics?

SHN: Since I am going to be dealing with this issue in the next lecture, I shall give only an abbreviated answer here. Metaphysics in the authentic sense, whether Islamic or Hindu or anything else, always deals also with epistemology. The roots of traditional epistemology are found in metaphysics; that is, the question of the subject who knows and how and what he or she can know are related to metaphysics. What happened in the West is that philosophers went from metaphysics to epistemology to logic to illogicality, if one includes existentialism, which tried to go against mere logical thought but in a "downward" manner, and now deconstructionism, which is part of postmodernism. These are the four stages that Western philosophy followed from the sixteenth and seventeenth centuries onward, but the case of Islamic philosophy is very different, for the Islamic tradition metaphysics contains the principles of epistemology. We can know metaphysics because there is something in us called the Intellect that can know things in principle and not just in their applications. I shall discuss this matter later because it is a very important issue and there is so much confusion surrounding it, including in the understanding of Heidegger who, although he uses the term *intellect* all the time and he knew Greek and Latin well, did not use it in the same traditional

10. Seyyed Hossein Nasr, *Islamic Philosophy from Its Origin to the Present: Philosophy in the Land of Prophecy* (Albany: State University of New York Press, 2006), 63–84.

sense as *nous* and *intellectus*. *Intellect* in its traditional sense does not have the same meaning as it has in modern philosophy, and it refers to both a microcosmic and macrocosmic reality. It is not the same thing as reason. There are many levels of the Intellect that modern philosophers, even Heidegger, simply refuse to consider, while in Islamic metaphysics, cosmology, and epistemology, higher levels of the Intellect are very significant. The higher levels enable the human being to know in a principial way and, in a sense, to know what is already written upon the tablet of the heart where the Intellect resides. The meaning of the famous *ḥadīth* "He who knoweth himself, knoweth his Lord" (*Man ʿarafa nafsahu fa-qad ʿarafa Rabbahu*) confirms this truth. Why is it that if I know myself, I know God? Because already the Reality of God is present at the center of my real self, and once I know myself in depth, by virtue of that knowledge, I gain knowledge of God. I shall deal with this matter more extensively soon.

Questioner 2: I am curious as to whether or not metaphysics addresses a paradox that I have wrestled with my whole life. It concerns the idea that when we look at the physical world, it seems that we can see what appear to be miracles happening. For example, in the past century or two, we see the inventions of the television, the airplane, the car, and so forth, and it seems as if we have moved away from metaphysics while witnessing all of these apparent miracles in the physical world. But paradoxically, what I understand from you and from metaphysics in general is that miracles happen in an inner dimension. Does metaphysics talk about that paradox?

SHN: First of all, you use the word *paradox*. What is the paradox? *Paradox* is a term that has to do with logic. When two contending truth claims cannot be logically included in a single assertion and yet one tries to do so, the result is a paradox. I do not see any miracles occurring these days except the "miracle" of the human destruction of the natural environment with the anticipated result that we are all going to suffocate before long. I do not see any "miracles" in modern science and technology around us, only miracles in reverse. Frithjof Schuon, the aforementioned remarkable sage who is read much less than he should be these days, once said so aptly that the modern world and the Greek world are miracles in reverse.[11] Everyone talks about the Greek miracle, but no one talks about the Indian miracle or the Persian miracle—only the Greek miracle. What happened in

11. Frithjof Schuon, *Sufism: Veil and Quintessence*, trans. Mark Perry et al. (Bloomington, IN: World Wisdom, 2006), 98.

classical Greece, however, is a miracle in reverse. I would not, therefore, use the word *miracle* in the case to which you refer. The modern world has invented many tools and gadgets, and in the field of pure science, quantum mechanics, if understood in light of traditional cosmology, has been able to gain an insight into the potential world that in fact underlies the already actualized world of subatomic particles. This statement is not so easy to understand for everyone, but it is a metaphysical and cosmological statement and has to be made. Furthermore, I do not see any logical paradox in the rise of secularism in the postmedieval West. What has happened is that the traditional spiritual world has been eclipsed and marginalized by modernism, and eclipse and paradox are two very different things. Yes, we live in a world in which authentic metaphysics is eclipsed in mainstream currents of thought. Modern Western civilization, and now its extension into other continents, marks the first time in human history when you can search everywhere throughout a city and rarely find a single sage who can teach you traditional wisdom.

Questioner 3: I use *miracle*, which I condition with *apparent*, because I cannot think of better words to use. I agree with what you are saying. Once spiritual knowledge is eclipsed, human civilization invents the airplane, the internet, and so on. To me, that is a paradox and again perhaps I am using that term incorrectly as well.

SHN: No, it is not a paradox at all. Every time a "heaven" is lost, a new "earth" is discovered by compensation with the help of the Devil, you might say. This is not my statement; it is something I once heard from Frithjof Schuon. It is one of the most remarkable statements that he made, asserting that there is a "compensation" for the loss of every "heaven" with the discovery of a new "earth." We are in the middle of one of those "falls" right now.

Cyberspace has provided modern man with a new shadowy world—that is, a deeper space within the Platonic cave that reflects only the shadow of the shadow of objective reality on its wall. It is a shadow of what Plato called the world of shadows. And tragically, many people live much of their lives in that shadowy world now. How often does one see at a party four people sitting together, but no one is talking with the others; they are all on their cell phones or laptops. This development does have certain compensations, even intellectual compensations; otherwise, it would not exist, but what is lost is greater than what is gained. It is true that you can look up the Song of Solomon in one minute on your phone and you can read it on the train, something that you could not do before, but this possibility has come at a heavy price. So, there is something that attracts one to these gadgets, but altogether they take a person to a lower level of reality. The fall of man is characterized by a series of such falls. With every fall has come the discovery of a new earth, an earth that appears to be filled with "infinite" new possibilities.

Look at what happened in Western Europe in modern times. Many Europeans turned from their own tradition, from Christianity. But at the same time, they captured the Americas and took over its wealth. They destroyed millions of Indigenous peoples, but they did not worry much about that fact and spoke of the New World as their own. They went to Australia, Africa, and other places around the world, and from their point of view, they discovered whole new continents and worlds while they were fast forgetting the beauty of their own medieval tradition. They forgot it so rapidly that it became as if it had never existed for them.

We see the result of this change everywhere in the West—for example, in the lack of spiritual beauty in the churches built only a few centuries after the Chartres Cathedral was built. What was created even for religious purposes is not traditional architecture functioning in a theocentric world; it is anthropocentric. The structures are completely humanistic and worldly, and yet they are supposed to be churches whose use of space should direct one's focus heavenward. Instead, inside many of them, one experiences the delusional grandeur of fallen man and not the majesty of God. I know many Christians who are put off by even the architecture of the Vatican itself. It is a sixteenth-century worldly palace and not the Christian architecture examples of which one sees in the Santa Maria Maggiore in Rome or the Notre Dame Cathedral in Paris. Those are examples of authentic Christian architecture. But this art became all but lost because a heaven was forgotten and a new earth discovered, you might say.

We find ourselves in the middle of a similar process right now. We are all duped, in a sense, by the ease with which we are able to navigate the cyber world. But we pay a heavy price. What has happened to human relations, our relation to nature, and our relation to God? Even family members speak directly to one another less than before because of their fascination with their devices such as cell phones and laptops. Thus, I do not think it is a question of a paradox at all. It is a question of a fall. Since we are human beings, it is always possible, however, to undo the effect of every fall. You can always return to the Source and Origin, to your true home. And one of the meanings of the Quranic saying *lā taqnaṭū min raḥmati'Llāh* (Q 39:53; Despair not of God's Mercy) is that there is always the possibility of this return. We do not have to participate inwardly in the fall just because we live in a particular day and age.

2

Metaphysics and the Domain of Contingency in Light of Metaphysical Knowledge

In this second of three lectures on metaphysics, I shall deal with why and how to study metaphysics. My discussion will begin with the issue of how we should study it. Although the question of how to study metaphysics is a difficult subject to delineate easily because of the diversity of human nature, there are certain constants to which one can allude.

First of all, as I mentioned in the preceding lecture, there are certain people who have a gift for metaphysics, people who are concerned with Ultimate Reality and who have an existential need to ask questions about Its nature. For most people, however, such questions are not of central importance in their lives. Among those who do have this gift for posing ultimate questions, there are those who have the gift, one might say the Divine gift, of being able to find answers that satisfy their minds and souls. We have to ask: What is it in the human microcosm, in man's very being or constitution, that enables one to understand metaphysics? Where does that ability come from? A great deal of discussion has taken place concerning these questions in various traditions, and they concur that ultimately, this ability comes as a gift from the Divine. For those who are inwardly attracted to metaphysics, the answer as to why they should study is that they have an existential need to do so. Their minds, souls, and hearts yearn for the principial knowledge that is their source of happiness.

The traditional understanding of what it meant to be man (I use the word *man* here and elsewhere in its generic sense as "human being," or *insān*, not as "male") became eclipsed in mainstream Western thought in the sixteenth and seventeenth centuries and is therefore absent in the worldview of modernism. Nowhere is this event clearer than in the French philosopher Descartes's reduction of intellect to reason and the division of reality into two dimensions, *res cogitans* and *res extensa*—that is, the realm of knowledge and the realm of extension. Regarding *res extensa*, he said that everything in nature is extension—that is, pure quantity—while *res cogitans* is reduced to reason. This bifurcation and reductionist view of nature is, in fact, the foundation of a purely quantitative science, one that puts aside all of nature's qualitative aspects.

For Descartes, the *res cogitans* dimension of reality is the thinking mind confined to man alone. Now, the word *mind* itself is problematic when translated into most non-Western languages. *Mind*, of course, has a historical Latin root, *mens*, but it is not the only element of human consciousness in the traditional understanding of human faculties. An Arabic speaker would be puzzled as to how to translate the English term *mind* into a single word in Arabic with the same range of meaning. Among the many books written in Arabic on the faculties of man, it must be asked why *mind* does not appear in any of them in the same sense of the word in English. The closest match in Arabic is *dhihn*, but in fact, that term refers to only one of the faculties of human consciousness. You have the words *khayāl*, or "imagination"; *istidlāl*, or "ratiocination"; the *ḥawās*, or the "various senses"; and so forth, but there is no word for mind in the modern sense in classical Arabic and Persian or other traditional languages.

What Descartes did was to collapse all the different cognitive faculties of man into a single "reality" called the mind, juxtaposed to matter, and this reduction heralded the beginning of rationalism. The logical consequence for anyone holding this view is that one should be able to understand everything through the use of human reason alone. In Descartes's famous hanging man argument, if a person were to be suspended in the middle of space without touching any object or any person, and if the hanging man had no sensation of contact with the world around him, he would still have an experience of himself. Therefore, according to Descartes, reality begins with the certitude of one's experience of oneself. This is the foundation of one of the greatest errors of human history if you look at it from a metaphysical point of view.

The Latin saying of Descartes, which is foundational to modern Western thought, is *Cogito, ergo sum* (I think, therefore I am). From the standpoint of tradition, including the Islamic, one would say, "I think, therefore God is"—that is to say, I can think and I can do so because there is God; He has given me the power of thinking. To say "I think, therefore I am," however, is to put thinking before being, whereas thinking is one of the functions of the human mode of being. In a sense, this atrophied view destroyed, once and for all, the meaning of the intellect as it is understood in Islamic metaphysics, in Hindu metaphysics, even in nontheistic Tibetan Buddhist metaphysics, and in any of the other traditional schools of metaphysics and epistemology.

We have to be able to navigate this difficult field. There is a great deal of error made by even some modern Muslim thinkers because they do not distinguish between the twin meanings of the word *ʿaql* in Arabic as both "intellect" and "reason." Its meaning depends on how you use it. The term, however, does not mean only reason; and Islamic philosophers are not rationalists because they use the word *ʿaql*. This kind of interpretation is based on a total misunderstanding, especially if one comprehends reason in its modern sense.

As for Islam, it never adopted the perspective of rationalism in its modern Western sense; otherwise, it would have ended up where the West found itself philosophically. In fact, it always rejected that perspective because in Islam, the divorce between reason and the intellect, which we see in the postmedieval West, never took place. There were one or two peripheral figures who tried to tread this path, but they had practically no influence. These include Ibn al-Rāwandī (ca. third/ninth century), for example, who was a scholar of Islamic thought, or perhaps even Abū'l-ʿAlāʾ al-Maʿarrī (d. ca. 449/1058), the blind Syrian poet, who was said to be a rationalist, even though that designation is somewhat far-fetched. In any case, these were not significant figures in the total tradition of Islamic thought. Ibn Sīnā was certainly not a rationalist. Even Ibn Rushd (known so well in the West as Averroes) was not a rationalist in the modern sense of Descartes and his like. So, the rationalist reduction to reason of our inner faculty of intellect—that light that is within us and that is so clearly described in the Quran and *Ḥadīth* where it is said, *al-ʿilmu nūrun* (Knowledge is light)—is a reduction that did not take place in the mainstream Islamic tradition. Muslims did not forget the *ḥadīth* of the Prophet that states that God has placed a light within us with which we gain real knowledge. The understanding of intellect in this sense has been completely forgotten in the modernist and postmodernist worldviews. Now, in order to understand how we can study metaphysics, we must first realize that there is a faculty in us that is appropriate to the study of metaphysics, and that faculty is *ʿaql*, *nous*, or *intellectus* in these terms' traditional senses, and it is through the use of this faculty that we can gain metaphysical knowledge.

The term *ʿaql*, which is found in various Islamic languages, is used also to mean being wise and practical in everyday life. Although it has many different usages in Arabic, the Quran identifies it primarily with the confirmation of *tawḥīd—hum lā ya ʿqilūn* (Q 2:171), referring to those who "do not understand [intellect]." This phrase should not be translated as "they do not reason." It is more accurate to translate it as "they do not intellect";[1] that is, they do not use their intellectual faculty to know *tawḥīd* or Divine Unity. To use *ʿaql* properly is to come to know and understand that God is One. The how of gaining metaphysical knowledge is using one's intellect as guided and enlivened by revelation. The Quran relates awareness of the truth of God being One not only with faith but also with intellection (*ta ʿaqqul*), *ʿaql* being the means to discern and understand principial truth. There is no such thing as Quranic rationalism, as some modernized Muslims falsely claim. For the sake of emphasis, let me repeat that *ʿaql* as understood traditionally is not simply reason in the modern sense.

It is very interesting to note that the word *ʿaql* in Arabic has the same root as *ʿiqāl*, which, like many Arabic roots, has something to do with the camel. It means to tether a camel, to tie a camel to something so that it does not run away. In the context of metaphysics, it means to bind our *ʿaql*, that noetic faculty that we have been given by God, to Him. The rich word *noetic* comes from Greek, and it is usually used in its adjectival form, not in its noun form. The term *noetic* is becoming more widely used of late in America and especially in California, where they are trying to revive some traditional sciences and where an Institute of Noetic Sciences has been established. The word *noēsis* itself, however, has not come into general usage in English, and although it was used occasionally during the English Renaissance and shortly thereafter, nowadays the adjective *noetic* is what is generally used. This term of Greek origin, from *noēsis*, which has the same meaning as *intellection* derived from the Latin *intellectus*, means a light that enables us to understand and gain knowledge of the Real, knowledge of the Self. In a sense, it is a knowledge that unifies, that brings about what is called *ittiḥād al-ʿāqil wa'l-ma ʿqūl* in Islamic metaphysics—that is, the unity of the knower and the known that occurs when the subject that knows becomes unified with the object that is known.

Now, in practice, although it is possible for some people to have metaphysical intuition, unless they belong to a tradition, unless the *nafs* is trained by the grace of revelation, that intuition usually wears away. So, for all practical purposes, there is no authentic metaphysics that is accessible in an integral manner outside of revelation, tradition, and religion. By *religion*, I do not mean simply the law and ethical considerations; I mean the total tradition. There is no in-depth exposition of metaphysics in the Islamic world

1. It is interesting to note that while in Arabic, *ya ʿqilūn* is still in usage, in English, the verb *to intellect* became discontinued in the modern period.

from Malaysia to Morocco without the Islamic revelation; there is no metaphysics in India without Hinduism; there is no metaphysics in China without either neo-Confucianism or Taoism; there is no metaphysics in the Buddhist world without Buddhism. There is no exception to this rule. One might ask, What about the Greeks? What about Aristotle himself or Plato? The answer is that they were heirs to the remnants of the Greek religion and its sapiential dimension. Greek philosophy was born from the cadaver of the dying Greek religion. The Orphic aspect of the Greek religion, its metaphysical aspect, was gradually dying out at the time of Plato, but from it was born Platonism and from that Aristotelianism and then Neoplatonism. The case of the Greeks can be seen externally to be an exception to the rule in a certain sense, the end result of which was the death of that civilization anyway. The people who really benefited from Plotinus were Muslims, Jews, and Christians, because the heart of the religion of ancient Greek civilization—and with it, the civilization itself—died soon after Plotinus.

Western scholars have tended to think of Greek philosophy as divorced from spiritual practice, but that is not true in a deeper sense. Parmenides says explicitly that it was not so, as did the other pre-Socratics. I shall not go deeply into a discussion of the term *philosophy* in general here, but being a student of philosophy, I have to say a few words about this topic. Let us remember that when Plato was asked "What is philosophy?" his answer was "Philosophy is the practice of death." Nothing could be further away from what is taught nowadays in courses on analytical philosophy at most Western universities. It is the philosophy expressed here by Plato that shows that even Greek philosophy is not an exception to what was mentioned above. Think of the words that Socrates spoke when drinking the hemlock, the poison that killed him. You could not find a single professor of philosophy in any Western university to take hemlock and speak in this way; so even Greek philosophy, if understood authentically, is not an exception to our assertion.

In the traditional world, metaphysics was always found at the heart of religion. In the West its language was drawn from the religious symbolism in the Abrahamic world, from the abstract language that came providentially from certain forms of Greek thought dating back to such early Christian thinkers and theologians as Origen (d. ca. 253) and Clement of Alexandria (d. 215) and also to some extent from ancient Egyptian thought as in Hermeticism. These philosophies developed in the Mediterranean world and allowed the three monotheistic religions—that is, the Abrahamic religions of Judaism, Christianity, and Islam—to have recourse to a shared philosophical language. It should be remembered that distinctly philosophical language came from

Greek and was used originally for both religious and metaphysical discourse and not what came to be known later as secular philosophy.

For Islamic thought the intellect is a faculty mentioned in the Quran as the faculty given by God to humanity in order to be able to know the One, the Ultimate Truth, and Its manifestation in relation to the Source of all existence. The Quran distinguishes very clearly between those who use this faculty and those who do not: *hal yastawī'l-ladhīna ya'lamūna wa'l-ladhīna lā ya'lamūna* (Q 39:9; Are those who know and those who do not know equal?). Clearly *'aql* is a fundamental concept in the Quran. There are also many *aḥādīth* pertaining to *'aql* as well. Moreover, Sayyidunā 'Alī has a famous saying, according to which the most precious thing that God created in the world was *'aql*, echoing the well-known *ḥadīth*, "The first thing that God created was the Intellect [*'aql*]." The outstanding intellectual figures of early Islam, Sunni and Shi'ite alike, emphasized the centrality of *'aql*, and this fact is especially true of those who have taught and expounded the inner dimension of Islam. They have made it known that *'aql* is the faculty by means of which we come to know the One, the Absolute, and therefore, it is the gateway and means of access to metaphysics, provided that it is "healthy" and in the state of surrender to God, that it is *al-'aql al-salīm* (the healthy intellect).

It is necessary here to open a parenthesis for those of you who may be thinking that Jalāl al-Dīn Rūmī, one of the greatest of all Islamic mystics, disparaged *'aql* when in his famous poem he said,

پای استدلالیان چوبین بود
پای چوبین سخت بی‌تمکین بود

The leg of the rationalist is a wooden leg;
And a wooden leg is very wobbly.[2]

"Did he really say this?" you may ask. Yes, he did. What he was criticizing, however, was precisely rationalism; he was speaking about what would be nearly equivalent to Cartesian reason, not Islamic *'aql*. That is why he also said, *'Aql-i juz'ī 'aql rā badnām kard* (The partial intellect [meaning reason] ruined the name of the [real] intellect).[3] This "ruining" is exactly what happened in Western civilization after the Middle Ages, and once the process of destruction finished, authentic metaphysics as I have described it in these lectures became completely marginalized and even rejected. The question of

2. Jalāl al-Dīn Rūmī, *Mathnawī-yi ma'nawī*, ed. R. A. Nicholson (Tehran: Amīr Kabīr, 1978), 3:2128.
3. Rūmī, *Mathnawī*, 5:463.

why and how to gain knowledge of this principial knowledge became irrelevant in the modern world.

Now, there is one more point to add to this emphasis I have placed on the use of *ʿaql*, this inner faculty within us, this inner eye—*ʿayn al-qalb*, "the eye of the heart," as the Sufis say, which we have to open, however difficult it may be. The eye is there but we have to open it through virtue, through love, through spiritual practice. Here I shall not go into the technical practices that are required to achieve this end. There is another element that is related to it, however, that must be mentioned. Although it might seem paradoxical to some, it has always existed in various religious climates, especially in the Abrahamic world, and that is the element of faith. In the Advaita Vedanta in the Hindu world, the situation is somewhat different, but the element of faith is not absent. Although gaining theoretical knowledge of metaphysics may appear to have nothing to do with faith, its realization, in fact, has everything to do with religious faith. Faith, in a sense, is participation in and acceptance of the "unknown." It is not a matter of faith to say, "I am now reading a lecture on metaphysics." That statement does not arise from faith; however, you have faith in your ability to stop reading the book that is in your hands and go out for a walk. In this case, you are anticipating something that is not there yet. Such anticipation is not intrinsic to understanding the theoretical aspect of metaphysics, and it is possible to *understand* metaphysics theoretically without having faith, but it is impossible to *realize* the truth of metaphysics without having faith. The realization of the truth of metaphysics always implies a credo; it requires *īmān* in the religious sense.

In Islam, there is often a play on words, in which Arabic is so rich. One example pertains to our subject here. Many Muslim thinkers have contrasted the metaphysics and gnosis of Islam to Greek philosophy by referring to the first as *al-ḥikmah al-īmāniyyah* and to the second as *al-ḥikmah al-yūnāniyyah*. There is a play here on the similarity between the word *yūnān* (Greece) and *īmān* (faith) while at the same time distinguishing between *al-ḥikmah al-īmāniyyah*—that is, a metaphysics based on faith—and the wisdom of Greek philosophy. Sometimes *yamāniyyah* is used in this phrase, which implies both Yemen and the East as well as the right hand. All these meanings are contained in the Arabic roots of these terms and are contrasted with *al-ḥikmah al-yūnāniyyah*. This expression illustrates that when it comes to the realization of the Truth, it is impossible to achieve it without faith, even though the theoretical understanding of it is possible. On a certain level, metaphysics is the highest science, and just as a mathematician can be a good or a bad person regardless of his or her skills as a mathematician, so too a good person or a bad person can be engaged in metaphysics on the theoretical level. It often happens, however, that a person of bad character will not be able to continue to be a serious metaphysician because his or her intuitions will soon fade or fall away. How many people have we seen in the twentieth century who wrote brilliant books when they were young but wrote only trivialities when they were fifty years old because they did not do anything with that intuition concerning principial knowledge that God had given them?

Having discussed briefly how to study metaphysics, I want to address the question, Why should we study metaphysics? Of course, for those for whom seeking answers to metaphysical questions is an existential need, the question does not arise. When I scratch my head, I do so because it is itching; I do not first ask myself why I am scratching it because this act is an immediate need. As soon as my head itches, I scratch it automatically. What we are asking philosophically, logically, however, is, Why spend time studying metaphysics? Does it make us better people? Does it allow us to go to Heaven? Does it make us earn more money? Does it make us love our children more? Why are we doing this? It is important to answer the very important question of why we study metaphysics because, I believe, the answer is pertinent for the wholesome life of humanity itself.

First of all, let me refer back to what was said in the previous lecture: No religion can survive fully for long without a living metaphysical tradition. This is not only my view but also that of many others. I say this not on conjecture but rather on the basis of having studied various religions for over half of a century, and I can attest to historical examples of this truth. The reason is very simple: Different human beings have different needs for causality. Usually between the ages of fifteen and seventeen, there occurs in the human being what traditional Islamic sources call "Divine attack," *al-ḥamlah al-ilāhiyyah*. This phrase refers to the phase in the life of most teenagers when they begin to think inwardly about God and other ultimate questions, even if for only a brief period of time. Most soon put these thoughts aside and focus their attention on mundane matters and distractions—nowadays, it is often computer games, but when I was young, it was mostly sports and various other worldly diversions. But a few of these young people cannot let the deeper questions go. These questions become existential, and they seek to find answers. In my case, when I was sixteen years old or even younger, I would stay awake all night long thinking of nothing but purely metaphysical questions: Where would I be if there were no Heaven and earth? Where and what is the origin of my being? Why can I not go back in my memory to the origin of my own consciousness? Where does it originate from? Most people do not bother asking these questions; certainly, they do not keep them awake at two o'clock in the morning. I mention this occurrence in my own life because it is important for you to realize that for metaphysically or mystically inclined people for whom these questions arise, there is no way forward in life unless they find answers in the same way that if you have pain in a muscle that prevents you from your favorite sport, you will keep searching until you find a doctor to cure the pain.

Among some believers in all religions, and even some brought up without a religion, there is an urge to find answers to ultimate questions. It is not unique to Arabs or Persians, Indians or Chinese and Japanese, or any other nationality or ethnicity of East or West. God has created such people in this way. Just as in every city of a million people there are a few fine painters, a few fine musicians, and so on, you also have a few people who have this kind of philosophical inner constitution and both aptitude for and need of authentic metaphysics. If their religion is going to keep them within its fold, it has to be able to provide answers for them, and that answer can never be simply "Obey your parents, be good, follow the law." That is all well and good on its level, but it does not answer why two and two is four. A logical question needs a logical answer. An ethical question needs an ethical answer, obviously. A question about love needs a response that has to do with love. Everything in life is like this. Only the like can respond to the like.

When a child asks a metaphysical question, in most families, the parents are unable to give an adequate response, nor can ordinary schoolteachers do so. How fortunate is the young person whose father or mother can answer his or her metaphysical and philosophical questions adequately. I was one of those fortunate children. My father was one of the greatest philosophers of Iran; every question that I had, he could answer. Many families do not, however, have such a person among them. So where can such a person go for answers? Traditional religions had created proper channels that provided answers to these fundamental questions on several levels remarkably well, from simple stories for children, mythological tales, poems with spiritual content that young people memorized, and so on, to full-fledged metaphysical teachings, all of which contain on a certain level the deepest responses in symbols, myths, or didactic expositions to these basic questions. I myself learned many Persian poems by heart at a young age, poems whose inner metaphysical content I realized only when I grew older. In the traditional world, as the child grew up a bit more—sixteen, seventeen, eighteen years old—gradually more intellectual and spiritual explanations were given to those who were seeking answers to the deepest questions, and so the religion was able to keep within its fold its most intelligent members.

It is very unfortunate that between the seventeenth and nineteenth centuries, not all but many of the most intelligent people in the West left religion in search of the truth elsewhere. This phenomenon did not usually happen among people of average intelligence; it happened most of all among people of high intelligence, including many well-known modern Western scientists and philosophers. Sir Isaac Newton (d. 1727), the father of classical physics, was a devout man with metaphysical inclinations, but in this domain, he was an exception among the scientists of his day, as was Kepler (d. 1630). Today, most Western scientists claim that they are agnostic or atheist in contrast to what we see in the cases of Newton and Kepler and a few other mathematicians, physicists, and chemists of the seventeenth century. Even Galileo (d. 1642) was not an atheist, and although he was a maverick against the church, he certainly believed in God. What happened to cause so many inquiring minds interested in science to leave the church during the following centuries? What happened is exactly what I said: Ordinary church teachings stopped being a source of metaphysical answers to many of the most profound existential questions that certain minds were seeking.

So, one might say that the first role of metaphysics is the preservation of religion itself. Whenever metaphysics is lost, religion gradually either exteriorizes itself—as is happening today in both Judaism and Christianity and now to a certain extent in Islam, Hinduism, and other religions with the rise of fundamentalism—or leads to skepticism and religious doubt. Also oftentimes, as has happened in the past, religion dissolves into magic or disbelief. In the West, theism becomes deism and then agnosticism. Such a decadence and dissolution happened with the Greek, Roman, Babylonian, Chaldean, and even Egyptian religions. The remarkable Egyptian religion that had prevailed for four thousand years, from what did it die? It died from magic. If you enter the incredible mausoleum of Ramses VI in Egypt, the power of magic is still palpable. The effect of this residue of magic has usually the most powerful effect on women more so than men. It might be added that it is not accidental that most women react to snakes more strongly than men do; the snake symbolizes psychic forces in mythology and possesses a psychic element.

It is essential to understand that religions cannot continue in a wholesome manner without the essential principial knowledge that is at their core. The case of Islam provides a living example of this truth. Today's disturbing acts of extremism that are done in the name of Islam are, in fact, blatant heresy that neglects the inner spiritual and metaphysical teachings of the religion. Islam needs its traditional treasure of knowledge now more than ever before, as do other religions. We can see that what is happening in certain quarters of the Islamic world is, in many ways, similar to what happened in the Christian world during the Renaissance and especially the seventeenth century. In much of the modern Islamic world, the most brilliant children are forced by their parents to study either modern medicine or modern engineering, even though many of them dislike the subject in which they are required to specialize. I have many friends who are exceptionally talented Iranian musicians but who are working as doctors in hospitals because they were compelled into that career by their parents. These types of careers have become the ideal in a majority of modernized Muslim families, and the negative consequence of this process is evident in much of Islamic society.

I was once the president of perhaps the most important scientific university in the Islamic world, Aryamehr University (now called Sharif University of Technology), whose educational standards are of such a high level that its successful graduates can get into Stanford University without an entrance examination. Upon becoming president, the first thing I did was create the department of humanities. I made this move because of my belief that the best students should not all be forced to study only science or engineering. What about the humanities and the arts? What about religion and philosophy? Nevertheless, despite my and others' efforts, the general trend continued toward more emphasis on modern science and technology and away from the humanities and religion. We can see the results before our eyes. Many of those students become fundamentalists, many of them modernists or even communists. Some among each group even turn to violence, something that I witnessed firsthand.

Most intelligent students among the Muslim youth who are in Western-style universities are, for the most part, no longer concentrating on Islamic studies, although there are exceptions. In Iran in recent years, there have been some very brilliant young students who have told me they tried to follow my trajectory, because I began as a physicist and ended up as an Islamic scholar. I have corresponded with or have met with many of them who, after having studied physics and mathematics, are now in Qom with a turban around their head studying Islamic thought, especially its philosophical and metaphysical aspects. I have also been in contact with a few students like them from Pakistan, Egypt, and other parts of Africa. By and large, however, the contemporary situation has become different from what existed in earlier days, when in every family in the Islamic world, the most intelligent young person would be led by the parents to study religion, as was also the case in the medieval West.

In the Islamic world, there is a looming crisis arising from the prospect of having mediocrity rule over society; that is, people not trained in the deepest wisdom and knowledge of the religion and its metaphysical foundation are ruling in many places over even our *ʿulamāʾ*. As recently as a century ago in the Islamic countries, and even today in some places in Muslim West Africa and Asia, the *ʿulamāʾ* were (and are) the most educated people in society.

They were not only the pious guardians of the religion; they were also the most knowledgeable intellectually. Now we have a whole army of Muslim doctors and engineers—many who have faith but are without the requisite knowledge—writing on the Quran, commentating on it as if doing so were a simple intellectual exercise, although they may indeed be competent professionals in their chosen fields of expertise. In other words, a great deal of what is written by Muslims on the intellectual and spiritual dimensions of Islam today comes from the pens of people who do not have enough inner knowledge and the depth of technical training in these matters to properly guide others. Consequently, the level of Islamic scholarship is coming down in many places, and this trend is a major challenge to the Islamic world.

There are some bright spots, however, in centers of learning that have recently been established, such as Zaytuna College in California, where some of the brightest students can go for Islamic studies. We owe it to God to keep such avenues open to them as they were to our ancestors. Their effort to maintain religious teachings at the most profound intellectual level is why we still have faith. If our great-grandfathers had consistently sent every one of their most intelligent children to the bazaar to become rug makers and merchants while sending those less intellectually gifted to become an *ʿālim*, there would be little of Islam left in the world today.

This diminution of the Islamic intellectual tradition is a major crisis that faces the Islamic world—in each place in a different way—but the important point is that without metaphysical knowledge, integral religions become lame and allow the door to be open to all forms of secularism and fundamentalism. Most religious *ʿulamāʾ* today have no answer to the challenge of secularism. Saying *Takbīr!* and *Allāhu akbar!* is not going to solve anything by itself. One has to answer incorrect thought with correct thought. One cannot answer intellectual challenges with emotions or by shouting slogans.

One of the greatest challenges to the Islamic world today is determining how to provide an intellectually appropriate Islamic answer to modern secularism. Even in the Islamic Republic of Iran, which was founded for the sake of Islam, there are many students today who are secularists. I regularly receive letters from students there who do not understand the Islamic point of view as it is being presented to them in public discourses. Certain questions that they have in their minds remain unanswered, and many in positions of authority are unaware of this lack of appropriate response from them and its severely negative consequences. Even a major Islamic country, Egypt, which has now become a military dictatorship, has its own set of reasons for the inability of its religious authorities to provide a metaphysical basis for the teachings of Islam, a basis that is absolutely necessary today.

In so many Islamic countries there is suffering as a result of the sense of loss of the healing effect of traditional wisdom, including where the Salafi and Wahhabi strains of Islam predominate and in which one is not supposed to ask profound questions. These shallow perspectives, based on the neglect or rejection of metaphysics and sapience, are certainly not helping cure the prevalent malady at all.

In this difficult situation in which we find ourselves, we would do well to learn something from what happened in the West. It is hard to understand why we Muslims are very good at learning every aspect of technology along with many cultural trends from the West, but when it comes to observing the West's significant failings, we are unable to avoid making the same mistakes. If a person saw that her sister had become ill from drinking water from a poisoned well, that person would avoid drinking there. Why is it that we never learn from the mistakes of the West resulting from the neglect of principial knowledge? I speak as a Muslim who has been devoted to Islamic causes his whole life, and I have to ask this question. What are we doing in copying blindly and forgetting our own traditions rooted in metaphysics? It is manifestly evident what has happened in the West, but we are insistent on making the same mistakes, especially when it comes to major intellectual and spiritual issues. The eclipse of metaphysics in the West brought about the weakening of religion and the rise of secularism, from the Renaissance and the Galileo trial to our own day. Christianity has been retreating step-by-step in so many domains in the face of the challenges that it confronts in the modern and postmodern worlds. Rarely does it take a step forward to refute the intellectual errors of modernism, and it is usually on the defensive intellectually. It is a religion that is reduced for many to loving God and one's neighbor but not asserting the truth found in metaphysics and traditional cosmology about the nature of Reality, the structure of the world, and the deep reasons why we should love God and the neighbor. When Christians do so here and there, their effort is immediately laughed off by the modern scientific establishment and its blind followers. I should add here that this situation is going to happen to Islam and Hinduism if great care is not taken to prevent it. In fact, it is already happening in certain circles in non-Western religious climates.

Now, having made this general statement, let me turn back to the central theme of sacred and secularized knowledge. Knowledge itself without authentic metaphysics—that is, without acceptance of metaphysical and noetic principles—has no choice but to become secularized. It becomes information rather than real knowledge. A civilization such as the Islamic that previously did not even have a word for secular (there is no word for secular in classical Arabic, in which everything is immersed in the sacred)[4] now finds itself becoming secularized in many ways, starting first of all with the domain of knowledge.

Let us return to the example of Muslim physicians and scientists who pray every day and are pious but whose professions have nothing to do with their piety except on the ethical level. Sapiential knowledge is not part of their lives even if they treat poor people well without asking exorbitant prices and lead a morally just life. Their training in medicine has nothing to do with Islamic metaphysics, science, philosophy, or theology. I have given a great deal of thought to this matter, having been placed in my life in situations where I had to face this issue directly. While in Iran, as the president of Sharif University of Technology and having had a background in science, philosophy, and theology, I was able to experience this dilemma directly and with open eyes. There is a lot in my heart that I would like to say on this subject, but I cannot do so publicly because it involves not only principles but also individuals about whom I do not wish to speak critically.

The truth of the matter is, however, that unfortunately, even governmental authorities in cultures that claim to be religious have practically no understanding of the dire consequences of mere secularized knowledge and the exclusion of sacred wisdom. In those still half-traditional worlds, universities exclude or belittle their own humanities, focusing almost solely on Western science and technology as well as secularized social sciences and humanities that have originated in the modern West.

What happens when metaphysics, philosophical and theological thought, and the traditional humanities are taken out of life's equation is that those who continue to practice their religion do so without giving thought to its inner meaning, and they also study and make a career in some modern field such as medicine and engineering without thinking of their effect on one's intellectual vision and soul. On what is engineering based? On what is modern science based? They are based on a worldview according to which the world is cut off from the Hands of God, a world in which the Nature of God is irrelevant. A devout Muslim can also be a good physicist, as in the case of Abdus Salam, who won the Nobel Prize in Physics. He considered himself a Muslim, one who prayed regularly, and won a Nobel Prize. Of course, a person can be an atheist and win the Nobel Prize in Physics, a fact that means that God is irrelevant to the whole modern scientific enterprise.

4. The term *ʿalmāniyyah* is a recent invention in the Arabic language to refer to secularism. It is related not to *ʿilm* (knowledge) but to *ʿālam* (world).

Why do we not admit this fact? Where are our Muslim thinkers, people whose worldview is firmly rooted in the sacred knowledge that we have inherited? While it is fine to take pride in the achievements of physicists who are Muslim and in the recognition that they receive for their work, we must ask, What does their work have to do with Islam? Put aside the West. One can see this problem everywhere. The Japanese are not Muslims, and look at what they have done in physics. Consider what the Chinese are doing. Hindu India has more fine mathematicians than all the Islamic world put together, but this fact has nothing to do with Hindu metaphysics and cosmology—nothing to do with the price of eggs in China, as the saying goes. The work being done in these other civilizations cannot serve as a model for us. We have to turn to our own tradition. Our modernized intellectuals, Islamically speaking, are like birds with broken wings because they are trying to delete the supreme science of the Real from their worldview and make it irrelevant, and this action, then, has an effect that permeates into everything around them, starting with knowledge itself, which becomes secularized.

This is the situation we are now facing in the Islamic world as well as elsewhere in the non-Western world. In Islamic countries, most universities that claim that their programs are based on *tawḥīd* are compartmentalized; half of their offerings are the same secular subjects that are offered in any Western university, and then courses from the *kulliyyat al-Sharīʿah,* the Faculty of Islamic Law, are thrown into the mix for good measure to show their concern for Islam. What has happened to the Islamic universities that many people, myself included, worked to establish in the 1960s and 1970s? What has happened fifty years later? Even the Islamic universities in Malaysia, in Nigeria, and in other locations are mostly copies of Western universities with a faculty of *Sharīʿah* added. Sadly, that is all we have been able to do so far. We have lost the unity of knowledge that is fundamental to Islamic civilization. In fact, there is nothing more fundamental in Islam than unity. Even the word *ʿulamāʾ*, as understood traditionally, reveals this universality and unity.

Today, however, in Arabic, *ʿulamāʾ* usually means "those with turbans who know Islamic Law." In the Arab world, it does also mean, to some extent, "those who teach physics at Ain Shams University," while in Persia and most other Islamic countries, the term is confined to scholars of religion. But even in the Arab world, the two types of *ʿulamāʾ* have little to do with each other intellectually; they are living in two different intellectual universes. In contrast, when Ibn Sīnā wore a turban on his head and was considered an *ʿālim*, he was seen as part of a class of people who had knowledge of various sciences, all of which were related. Although some had more of a specialization in Islamic Law, some in grammar, some in history, some in medicine, some in mathematics, whatever it may be, they were each known as an *ʿālim* because each had mastery over an aspect of a science based on unity, one that was rooted in sacred knowledge. It is the knowledge of this underlying unity that has now been lost to a great extent and needs to be rediscovered.

* * *

Concomitant to what I have said, it is necessary to say a few words about the question of the metaphysical foundations of traditional Islamic art and the crisis created by its neglect. Traditional art, at whose heart lies sacred art, has a metaphysical and cosmological foundation in all traditional civilizations. Nowadays, many people think that art is a luxury, that it is reserved for the wealthy who, after having achieved material success, can then afford to buy a second-rate Western naturalistic painting, or a piece of "mirrored calligraphy," or letters of the Arabic alphabet repeated as a pattern without any meaning. Of course, that is not authentic Islamic art but something else, a subject that I have treated in other writings. Islamic art is not a luxury. It is a matter of life itself. Why? Consider the *ḥadīth* "Verily God is Beautiful, and He loves beauty" (*Inna Allāha jamīlun, yuḥibbu'l-jamāl*). Now, if God is Beautiful and loves beauty, to create works that are ugly is to create things that God does not love, and that activity and its results, therefore, distance man from God. It is as simple as that. Have you ever thought that even now, if you go among the few Bedouins who still remain in Arabia or the Tuareg of southern Algeria, who live very simply in the desert, how beautiful everything is with which they surround themselves? Their tents are made beautifully, as are the carpets inside. Carpets woven by nomads can be found rarely on the market in Western cities, and when one is found, it is snatched up immediately.

As for the built environment created by the sedentary Muslims, beautiful forms are found all the way from Moulay Idriss in Morocco to the Shalimar Gardens in Pakistan, and from the Jāmiʿ Mosque of Isfahan to the great mosques of India and the Sultan Hasan Mosque in Cairo. One finds thousands of remarkable buildings, from mosques to bazaars to palaces and everything in between, throughout the traditional Islamic world. I am not saying that the Islamic civilization is the only one to have created remarkable art. What I am saying is that the basis for the emphasis on art in Islam is found in its spiritual structure, wherein God manifests Himself primarily as beauty even over goodness, in a certain sense, from which it is, however, never separated. The two are, in fact, united as revealed by the fact that in Arabic, as well as in Persian and other Islamic languages, the word *ḥusn* means both "goodness" and "beauty," and so Islam refuses to even separate the two. It is remarkable what this one word reveals about the whole philosophy of Islam concerning art and beauty.

This art pervaded and was pervasive; it was everywhere and always combined beauty with utility. It was not even called art in the modern sense, as shown by the fact that the root of the term *ṣanʿah*, or "making" in general, had to do with *ṣināʿah*, or what is called art today, as well as the making of things, preserving what has been lost in the West, where the word *ars* in Latin also means "to make," even though that meaning is not evident in the term *art* today. One of the Names of God in Islam is *al-Ṣāniʿ*, or the Maker. Traditional Muslims still remember that it is God Who has given us the power to make, and this recognition has manifested itself through all the traditional Islamic arts, both plastic and sonoral, including oral arts such as poetry and music. Even as recently as a little over a century ago, although it is hard to imagine now, a person walking through an Islamic city would hear beautiful sounds—the sound of the *adhān*, of a song being sung by someone in a shop, of someone playing a flute. Beautiful sound was everywhere, as were beautiful plastic forms. What a contrast to the noise and forms of Tehran or Cairo today. What have we done to ourselves in a hundred years?

We must ask ourselves, Why was this done? The answer is that we came to forget that Islamic art is a way to make manifest the deepest aspects of the religion—aspects that are even deeper than the legal ones—through forms that save the soul. These forms may be created by those who do not fully understand the metaphysics that underlies them, but they are based on metaphysics nonetheless.

How is Islamic art created? Why is ʿAlī called the founder of calligraphy in Islam by both Sunnis and Shiʿites? Why was he also often called the first Muslim metaphysician for his *Nahj al-balāghah* (*The Path of Eloquence*), which is the first book of metaphysical content in Islam after the Quran itself? Of course, the Quran is not a book of metaphysics in the ordinary sense; it is a sacred scripture, but it contains the deepest metaphysical teachings. My own teacher ʿAllāmah Ṭabāṭabāʾī (d. 1981) once wrote a book called *ʿAlī and Metaphysics* that is now available in a less-than-completely-satisfactory English translation. The text of ʿAlī has nothing to do with the legacy of ancient Greece or of any other civilization to which Islam was heir. It comes from the Quran and *Ḥadīth*. It shows, therefore, the centrality of this form of knowledge from the very beginning of the Islamic tradition. Moreover, it is not accidental that he is also considered the founder of Islamic calligraphy, the most important form of sacred Islamic art along with architecture. Metaphysics and art meet in ʿAlī's eloquent words and writings.

Throughout the centuries, there was a nexus between metaphysical and cosmological knowledge, the geometry that related to them, and plastic arts on one hand and sonoral arts on the other. The vast majority of great Islamic metaphysicians were poets, including those of the highest rank, such as Ibn ʿArabī and Jalāl al-Dīn Rūmī. Prior to the twentieth century, most of the classical music of the Islamic world was cultivated by Sufis and was underpinned by a complete cosmology and metaphysics. Indeed, the role of classical music in the Islamic world is to lead us to God. To quote the remarkable Jalāl al-Dīn Rūmī again:

مطرب آغازید پیش ترک مست
در حجاب نغمه اسرار الست

The musician began to play before the drunken Turk,
Behind the veil of melody the mysteries of the Eternal Covenant [asrār-i alast].[5]

Here the drunken Turk symbolizes a person drunk with the elixir of principial knowledge, and "Behind the veil of melody the mysteries of the Eternal Covenant [*asrār-i alast*]" refers to the covenant made between all of us, all the progeny of Adam, and God in pre-eternity before the creation of this world.

The Quran says, *alastu bi-rabbikum* (Q 7:172), with *kum* ("you" in the plural rather than "thee" in the singular) showing that the question is addressed to all of us and not only to Adam. The verse is "Am I not your Lord?" not "*thy* Lord," not *alastu bi-rabbika*, in the second-person singular. And we, all men and women of every age and clime, answered collectively, *balā* (Yea). We all participated in that response and made the pre-eternal covenant with Him. Hence the verse continues with *qālū balā*, not *qāla balā*, meaning that all of humanity said "yea" and that "yea" is witness to the eternal covenant with God that we have all made. Happy are those who keep that covenant! When Rūmī says, therefore, that music unveils the mysteries of this covenant with God, no higher praise could be given to an art; no art could hold a loftier position than that. This poem indicates the nature of the spirit of Islamic civilization, whether that civilization refers to Persians, Arabs, Turks, West Africans, Indo-Pakistanis, Malays, or otherwise.

Once a concert featuring Sundanese music was given in my honor in Java, in the city of Bandung. It is an exquisitely beautiful Sufi musical tradition that has been preserved for centuries, and it is a genre of music that I had never heard prior to that time. Tragically, much of this kind of spiritually rich music

5. Rūmī, *Mathnawī*, 6:703.

is now being lost or distorted right before our eyes. This phenomenon is yet another example of what happens when the metaphysical center is lost.

At the height of Muslim civilization, there was always a great master of the arts, whether it was in tile making, miniature painting, or music, whose intellect and heart were rooted in the metaphysical foundation of that art. That person was usually a master of the art in question who had learned the metaphysical knowledge involved from a spiritual master, or shaykh, and who would apply that knowledge to his art, which his students would then learn. It is that transmission of metaphysical truth that is now disappearing from many circles among us.

* * *

Then besides traditional knowledge and art, there is the necessity for ethics, without which no society can survive. Many Western philosophers claim that one can have operative secular and nonreligious ethics. One can find this claim in many of the books that are prevalent throughout the Western world. Over the past few centuries, in fact, some influential books have come out about non- or antireligious philosophical ethics, and since Thomas Hobbes in the seventeenth century, many Westerners have been writing about ethics divorced from religion. I do not want to discuss the Western case here, but can you imagine what the reaction would be to the divorce between religion and ethics in any Islamic city, even a large modern one where there are a lot of educated and Westernized people, such as my own city of birth, Tehran? If a professor of philosophy at Tehran University, where I taught for twenty years, were to go into the street in front of the campus and announce, "I have shown through philosophy that ethically it is wrong to, let us say, step on an ant that is crawling on the sidewalk," nobody would listen to him. If, however, a religious scholar or *ʿālim* were to come and say that stepping on an ant is against Islamic Law, most would heed his advice. Why is it that the secular government of a Muslim country could not have the same effect as the *ʿulamāʾ* among the general population?

When it comes to the question of ethics, even now with the spread of modernism, few listen to political figures in positions of power, but most Muslims still listen to the *ʿulamāʾ*. Muslims still listen to the religious scholars, the foundation of whose science is sapiential knowledge, the metaphysics of which I am speaking. If that basis disappears, it is very hard to make even ethical injunctions efficacious and to retain certitude even in the domain of actions. The traditional philosophical basis becomes forgotten, and with that loss comes either what we call a *taʿabbudī* attitude—that is, simply willful acceptance with no understanding as to why one should do certain things—or a rejection of the practices prescribed by religion. Doing things only because one's father said to do so leads to a great deal of the hypocrisy that we see so much of nowadays in the Islamic world, where a person practices an ethical norm in public, but not really believing in it, he or she does something quite different in private. This situation has done much harm to Islamic culture and society as well as to other traditional societies and cultures.

There is a direct link between ethics and metaphysics, and in Islamic civilization, nowhere has it been brought out more clearly than in Sufi texts. *Al-Risālah al-qushayriyyah* of Imām al-Qushayrī (d. 465/1072), one of the greatest treatises of Islamic and Sufi ethics, shows this link very clearly, as do the writings of al-Ghazzālī and others. Moreover, what happened in Islamic civilization is that after the Mongol invasion, in many places Sufi ethics, in a sense, breathed new life into Islamic ethics in general, and it became the norm for Islamic ethics overall. That is why even today when you come out of the al-Azhar Mosque in Cairo after the Friday prayers, you will find that the books on ethics that are being sold by nearby booksellers are almost all by Sufis such as Imām al-Qushayrī, al-Ghazzālī, Zarrūq (d. 899/1493), or someone like them. A text on ethics written by *fuqahā'* (jurisprudents) is read these days by only a few people, just a few Salafis and others like them, but traditional Islam was imbued with Sufi spirituality, which kept the Sufi texts and the link of ethics to metaphysics alive—that, and, of course, the example of saintly people. Nothing is more effective in leading a person to follow an ethical life than the example of a human being who is ethical. Just to talk about ethics is not enough; the example of individuals who are trained in metaphysics, who are usually members of Sufi orders, and who accomplish remarkable feats spiritually and ethically is also required. Without metaphysics, ethics loses its spiritual mooring and usually becomes weakened.

* * *

One of the most important debates that is going on in the Western world today and that now has permeated the Islamic world is the one between religion and modern science. From the time that Jamāl al-Dīn Afghānī (d. 1314/1897; more correctly, Jamāl al-Dīn Asadābādī) began to write on this matter in the nineteenth century, as did Muḥammad ibn Aḥmad al-Iskandarānī (d. ca. 1306/1888) in Egypt and several others until now, the issues surrounding religion and science have become the subject of major debates among Muslims. Most modern Muslims, impervious to the metaphysical foundation of the traditional sciences, say something like the following: Modern science is *'ilm*; God has said to seek *'ilm* even if it be in China and from the cradle to the grave. Therefore, since learning and cultivating science is a religious act, there is no dichotomy between religion and science in Islam. The usual discussion in modernized circles goes along these lines to this day.

To cite an example: Several decades ago there was a conference on the future of science in Pakistan in which Farooq Leghari (d. 2010), who was at that time the president of Pakistan, was present. We both spoke at the opening session. When I presented my views on Islamic science and opposed strongly the uncritical and wholehearted acceptance by some Muslims of modern science and its worldview, he put aside his paper in front of everybody and began to speak in order to refute what I had said. I will not go into the details of that story, but what he said typifies the attitude of most Muslim political authorities toward the religion and science question. Perhaps some of you reading these lectures will take up the mantle of defending the authentic Islamic understanding of science and its relation to religion. It is hard to believe, but many Muslims do not even understand what the problem is. Why is it that such a large percentage of Japanese have become secular and agnostic since the Second World War, in a land where Buddhism and Shintoism had been so strong before? The prewar military figures of Japan were nearly all Shintoists, and the emperor had a sacerdotal function; what happened? Nor is Japan alone among non-Western cultures to experience such a phenomenon of rapid secularization with blind acceptance of modern science. It is a subject that is rarely addressed in sufficient depth, but the subject of how religion and science are related to each other in traditional societies, on the one hand, and in the modern world, on the other, is a very important one that cannot be avoided.

Let us stop thinking about a facile, harmonious wedding of the two that many claim exists and instead think of where there are points of contention and principial opposition. It is the limitations of modern science that have to be understood. We have to comprehend that in light of authentic metaphysical teachings, it is neither truthful nor feasible for modern science simply to overrun the territory of religion one step after another. Modern science is now reaching inside the human brain and trying to reduce the human person to an automaton while attempts are being made to create life in test tubes. It appears that proponents of such efforts want to continue on this path until there is nothing left of the sacred presence in God's creation. These so-called advances are not going to achieve the ends planned for them, but the way they are being hailed as great achievements and breakthroughs makes it seem as if modern science is just on the verge of explaining everything in existence, thus making religion, and of course metaphysics, redundant—which is totally absurd.

I shall address this issue in depth in the next lecture, but what is very important to understand here is that what is missing in this whole discussion is metaphysics. Only metaphysics can reveal the principles of all authentic science, including providing insight into the usually unstated presumptions of modern science. What are the limitations of modern science? What does it mean when we reduce an apple falling from a tree onto Newton's head to mass and motion and the gravitational field of the earth? What have we done in this reductionism? These are important issues, extremely important issues, which only metaphysical knowledge and traditional cosmologies derived from it can answer.

Metaphysical knowledge is also essential for the understanding of the deeper causes of the environmental crisis. I have dealt with this issue in so many of my works, such as *Man and Nature* and *Religion and the Order of Nature*, that I shall not go into it again here.[6]

* * *

To come back to art before I end this section of my discourse, we have to remember that what happened in the modern West was a gradual humanization and finally dehumanization of art, especially sacred and traditional art. Even Christ began to be painted in the postmedieval West as just a handsome man with a long beard—of course, often he was depicted as blond, but that is beside the point—and the Virgin Mary as an innocent-looking woman in an ordinary, humanized form far removed from the Black Madonnas of the Middle Ages. In *The Marriage of the Virgin*, the famous early sixteenth-century Italian painter Raphael depicts Mary based on the model of a young girl from Florence. In contrast, the medieval paintings of the Virgin often have elongated, dark faces and do not look naturalistic at all. It is those stylized paintings, however, that are sources of miracles for Christians, not the painting of the pleasant-looking Italian girl. Such naturalistic paintings may look pleasing to our untrained eyes, but what happened in Western Christianity was that there took place a humanization of sacred art; that is, images of God, Christ, the Virgin, and the paintings and sculptures of saints were also naturalized and humanized. Once that happened, it took only a short time before Western art became *de*humanized in the twentieth century, when even the natural image is rejected from below rather than above. Even as pious a French painter as Rouault (d. 1958) painted images of Christ in a kind of form that falls *below* naturalism. This style is often called *surnaturelle* or *surréaliste*, but it is not really surrealist; it is subrealist because it falls below

6. Seyyed Hossein Nasr, *Man and Nature: The Spiritual Crisis in Modern Man* (Chicago: ABC International Group, 1997); Seyyed Hossein Nasr, *Religion and the Order of Nature* (New York: Oxford University Press, 1996).

the ordinary realism of naturalistic art, to which I just referred in speaking of the humanization of Christian art.

Now, fortunately, in Islam, we do not have sacred images of God and the Prophet, so we are saved from this particular form of decadence; but we do have the humanization and naturalization of traditional art occurring in certain forms of art in the Islamic world. You might ask, What does this have to do with metaphysics? It has to do with the loss of vision of the metaphysical foundation of traditional art that ends up with this downward spiral. Why is it that these days, so many people coming from Arabia and other wealthy Islamic countries have the most decadent form of furniture in their houses, the kind of gilded, pseudo–Louis XIV furniture that is found in stores on Edgware Road in London, where it is sold almost exclusively to rich Muslims; no Englishman would be caught dead buying something like it. Why are we doing this? I might add, however, that simple Scandinavian furniture, which happens to be more like Islamic furniture because of its simplicity and purity, is now bought by a few Muslims, and IKEA stores selling Swedish furniture have been gaining some popularity in certain Muslim countries.

Even some Persian carpets, among which one finds a number of the greatest masterpieces of Islamic art, are now beginning to look more and more naturalistic in their patterns. What has happened to all of our geometric designs, those incredible symbolic patterns of Islamic art? I am not saying that they are totally absent because traditional Islamic art still survives, but in many instances, the colors are becoming more and more gaudy while the forms are becoming less and less traditional and evermore naturalistic.

So, we are now able to see throughout much of the Islamic world—and, I might add, throughout other still predominantly traditional societies—the immediate impact of the loss of the sacred in art, be they ugly buildings, or houses of worship, or the furniture in people's homes. In the Islamic world, an art that has remained traditional is the carpet, which is still, for the most part, handmade, but as I just mentioned, even there one sees patterns that are becoming more naturalistic and less symbolic. Good carpets are still being produced, but on the whole, the quality is worsening in many places due not only to social and economic factors but above all to the loss of the traditional worldview that is based ultimately on the metaphysical knowledge of reality. What I have said about carpets applies also to calligraphy, architecture, and other forms of Islamic art.

Many Muslims go to the West or receive Western-style products that they then emulate. The blind imitation of the Western style of living by the wealthy in the Islamic world through their purchases and sponsorships is contributing to the degradation of the traditional arts throughout the region, and that degradation is one of the greatest tragedies. Every art needs a patron. In the old days, the great patrons of all Islamic art and architecture were either royal courts, rich merchants, the *'ulamā'* when it came to mosques and *madrasahs*, or the Sufi orders. What happened from the nineteenth century onward is that the *'ulamā'* and Sufis became less wealthy and could no longer easily support big projects, although there were exceptions. The merchant class became richer still, but its taste in art became more and more Westernized at the same time. Members of the royalty and the aristocracy, who had supported high art, were the first to become Westernized; thus, the patronage for traditional art weakened greatly, and gradually, the taste for the traditional arts was lost in these upper classes as well. There are, of course, some notable exceptions, as we see in the case of Sultan Hasan of Morocco and Empress Farah of Iran. This change first began in Türkiye and Egypt, then it was seen in Iran and among some Muslims of India before it spread to other areas. The phenomenon happened later and to a lesser degree in certain countries such as Yemen and Oman, for example.

This complicated phenomenon had many causes, but most of all it was the result of the loss of the knowledge of principles, knowledge of the metaphysics and cosmology that are the foundations of traditional and sacred art and their symbolism. In a like manner the loss of the traditional worldview that makes ethical actions meaningful in an ultimate rather than arbitrary sense has occurred in many quarters. There are certain religious proscriptions that are hard to understand, such as abstention from pork even if it is medically safe. Ordinary Muslims follow the religious injunction because, for them, it comes from God, but that way of acting becomes weakened if the cosmological and metaphysical reasons are forgotten. One should try to apply one's intelligence in order to understand the laws, and in fact, it is the religion itself in its sapiential dimension that always provides the means of understanding the why of its injunctions. It is not that people of old all had stronger faith than ours and therefore they never drank and they never ate pork. No, it was that usually such religious injunctions were explained much more clearly to those in need of explanation than they are to most of the people of our generation.

* * *

Once again, I ask this question: Why do we need metaphysical knowledge? I shall repeat some reasons but shall do so from another perspective to make sure that this truth is understood. First of all, we need metaphysical knowledge in order to preserve authentic religion itself. No traditional religion can survive intact for long without authentic knowledge of Ultimate Reality and the ability to present a comprehensive vision of It. The Quran mentions Heaven and Hell repeatedly, but how do we know these exist? Either we accept that they exist because we have faith in the Quran or we begin to question their existence. The latter is the case of some young Muslims today who no longer believe in traditional eschatology because they do not understand its metaphysical necessity. There has to be a metaphysical perspective in each tradition available to those who are in need of it. If this were a longer lecture, I could explain here why there have to be paradisal and infernal states of being, why states of being have been created in such a way as to extend from the most perfect state of being through descending orders to the lowest realm, why there has to be manifestation or creation, and why once there is creation, there is already separation from God. Since only God is absolutely Good, the separation from God is what then appears as evil, and Hell is separation from God, metaphysically speaking. Most human beings need this simplified explanation; otherwise, even the inner meaning of the language of the Quran becomes difficult to understand, and people fall into the danger of selecting certain verses for their convenience and neglecting others.

Thus, our primary objective should be to preserve and resuscitate this principial knowledge. Now, God has not only given us oil, which a former president of Yemen once called the urine of the Devil (and he was not completely wrong because it has done more harm to many of us compared to the good it has brought), but He has also enabled us to gain access to an unbelievable treasury of knowledge embedded in our traditional sources. Few traditions, including especially those of the West, have as many works that are devoted seriously to metaphysics in the real sense of the term as has Islam, where this wisdom is expressed in the forms of poetry as well as prose, in both symbolic and abstract language. In this field of *ḥikmah*, there are a vast number of treatises written in diverse languages for all the different audiences for which they were meant. We need some heroes to resuscitate these works and must not leave the task in the hands of orientalists who publish texts with a thousand outward criticisms that often make them opaque to our young people who can really benefit from such works if they are presented authentically and in a contemporary language.

It is astonishing how rich this genre of writing is, not only in Arabic and Persian, but also in Turkish and Urdu that came later as well as in Bengali, Punjabi, and many other languages, but especially the two major Islamic languages, Arabic and Persian. There are hundreds upon hundreds of extraordinary treatises, but only a small percentage of them are readily available even in the original language, not to speak of translations. Young people in Canada or in America are not to be blamed if they cannot read a centuries-old

Arabic or Persian text. It is the duty of scholars to make such works readily available, but unfortunately, we have not been completely successful so far. Some Muslim countries are in a somewhat better situation than others when it comes to the number of texts translated; but still, it is difficult to gain access to many of them.

Kemal Atatürk's (d. 1938) change of Turkish orthography from the Arabic-Persian alphabet to the Latin alphabet was one of the greatest cultural disasters of Islamic history. He said that within a few years, every worthy Ottoman work would be available in the new alphabet, but now close to one hundred years later, the majority of such works have still not been published in the Latin-based alphabet, let alone been translated into other languages. So, the Turks are missing a major part of their seven-hundred-year intellectual heritage. There is a movement in Türkiye now calling for teaching Ottoman Turkish in schools. If implemented, this policy—which, as a friend of the country, I have been advocating for over fifty years—would be a major transformation not only in Türkiye but also indirectly in some other parts of the Islamic world. Unfortunately, we are sleeping over treasures.

It is not that difficult to change course given that the availability of many young scholars for this task and the financial means to support their work both exist. Instead of encouraging all our gifted young students in the modern educational system to make the most money possible by becoming doctors and engineers, let us encourage and facilitate a program for at least 10 percent of them to study the Islamic humanities and related subjects.

I have always said that in this matter, we should learn from the Jewish people. When the large Jewish migration to America took place, many big Jewish families had at least one son who became a rabbi or scholar of Judaism, one son or daughter a doctor, one a lawyer, one a businessman—not all became engineers and doctors. The result is that now, practically every major chair of Jewish studies in America is held by a Jewish scholar, as it should be.

But that is not our case, unfortunately. There are approximately seven million Muslims in the US, and they include a highly educated class that is already becoming a notable presence in many fields such as medicine, but as far as Islamic studies is concerned, there is a long way to go, although some progress has been made, and there are now a notable number of fine young Muslim scholars of Islamic studies in American universities from Harvard to UCLA. It is remarkable what Muslim doctors have achieved, but from the point of view of the topic under discussion here, this phenomenon alone is not sufficient. Now is the time, when we have so many professionals in different fields and considerable wealth at our disposal, to fund far-reaching programs that make traditional metaphysical knowledge as expounded over the centuries accessible to those qualified to understand it and especially to our young people in a language that they can comprehend.

Then besides the task of preserving religion itself in an authentic form, one of the most important roles of metaphysics at this juncture in history should be in preventing the negative, secularized forces issuing from the modern scientistic worldview from destroying Islamic intellectuality completely. It is said jokingly by some that, fortunately or unfortunately, in some Islamic countries, modern science is taught so badly that it is not a threat to Islamic intellectuality; therefore, there is no need to worry. In some countries, however, including Iran, whose situation I happen to know only too well, Sharif University of Technology has produced some of the most brilliant scientists in the world. Many of them are now professors in places such as MIT, Stanford, and Harvard. There are many very gifted people from that country as well as from other parts of the Islamic world who should be living and teaching in their home countries but who, in fact, are fleeing from there, partly because they have adopted worldviews that have nothing to do with their culture and partly for political and social reasons. Many of them come from pious families and are practicing Muslims, but that is not enough, for they do not feel an intellectual attachment to their own intellectual tradition and are not aware of the destructive effect of secularized science, which is much more pervasive than our rationalistic, fundamentalist friends would make us think. How interesting it is that fundamentalism and modernism are united in so many domains, such as indifference to the destruction of Islamic art and neglect of the role of a secularized science in a religious society. In fact, they encourage—intentionally or unintentionally—secularizing tendencies along with many other disruptive attitudes. Consequently, we have, of course, a very big battle to face to preserve the primacy of principial knowledge, at whose heart resides metaphysics understood traditionally.

There is also the crucial need for metaphysical knowledge in the preservation of traditional and sacred art everywhere, including in the Islamic world. Fortunately, the last forty to fifty years have seen a certain amount of positive movement, especially in Islamic art and architecture. Starting about five decades ago, there began a semblance of a movement to try to preserve and revive traditional Islamic art from architecture to calligraphy, thanks to the works of people such as Titus Burckhardt (d. 1984) and Jean-Louis Michon (d. 2013), both of whom were Western Muslims, and of course some Muslim architects from within the Islamic world, namely Hassan Fathy (d. 1989) and his students, such as Abdel-Wahed El-Wakil (b. 1943) and Omar El-Farouk (b. 1942), a group in Iran with which I was closely associated in days of old, and groups in other places such as Morocco. Of all the different fields of endeavor, this one is perhaps the most successful and fruitful. We have now several schools of traditional Islamic art and architecture, including the School of Traditional Arts founded by King Charles III in London, which has a strong Islamic art component, and the College of Traditional Islamic Arts in Amman, which is based on that model and trains traditional Islamic craftsmen and architects based on Islamic, philosophical, and metaphysical foundations. There is also a major school of this character and perspective in Lahore founded by Kamil Khan Mumtaz called the Hast-o-Neest Institute of Traditional Studies and Arts. In the next lecture, I shall return to the relation between metaphysics and the cosmological sciences and how the traditional sciences relate to traditional art.

Turning again to religious ethics, it must be pointed out that traditional religious ethics has been under attack in modernized circles, especially over the last few decades. Even in a place such as Chechnya, where the Sufi orders that had survived seventy years of ruthless communist rule have begun to succumb to the well-financed, oil money–funded campaigns that spread a fundamentalist viewpoint that divorces ethics from metaphysics, this viewpoint can be seen to be succeeding in some places where the Communist Party and often externally funded fundamentalism failed. However, even in such places, there is still a thirst for Sufi ethics, which is essential to understanding the inner significance of Islamic ethics in general, and Sufi orders are being revived in Caucasia as well as in Türkiye itself. There is also a great deal of interest in this issue in Iran and Afghanistan and even in some parts of the Arab world, despite the spread of Salafism in those regions, as well as in some countries in Africa, including Nigeria, Mauritania, and Morocco, where there is strong devotion to religious ethics in its relation to mysticism and metaphysics. The same situation holds true in South and Southeast Asia.

The revival of a deeply rooted Islamic ethics combined with a renewed understanding of metaphysics can have the deepest effect by making the formulation of ethics appeal to both intellect and faith. If a person adheres to ethics because the Quran has said to do so or because his or her father has said to do so, a time may come when that person does not understand why he or she is doing certain things; then that element of questioning in the mind begins to take over and can have very negative consequences religiously. Many of you have felt this temptation; Shayṭān is always around. We might be asleep, but he is always awake, and a religious ethics rooted in both faith and metaphysics is the best bulwark to protect the soul and mind of the faithful against the demonic.

There are certain other domains that might not seem to be as central to many but are, in fact, very important and where the need for a renewed understanding of metaphysics is essential. For example, today there is a great deal of interest in many circles in the West in "spirituality" rather than religion. In the West many people do not talk about religion anymore, but they consider themselves proponents of spirituality. In places such as California, which one might say sets the "fashions" in this field, spirituality is very fashionable while religion is not, although how there can be spirituality without religion is not made clear. In any case, when the term *spirituality* is translated into Islamic languages—for example, as *rūḥāniyyah* (Arabic) and *maʿnawiyyat* (Persian)—it is associated with Sufism, gnosis, metaphysics, and related realities. In fact, intellectuality and spirituality are inseparable from each other in Islam, although this is not so in most prevalent currents of Christianity. In the Islamic perspective, authentic intellectuality and authentic spirituality are interrelated, and so, of course, the revival of one requires the revival of the other, both of which we need so much in the Islamic world today. We need people like those in ages gone by who wrote on the revivification of the sciences of religion, people such as al-Ghazzālī, who revived Islamic ethics from within by turning to Sufism and metaphysics. We need to have this task carried out again and to bring up the question of the revival of authentic Islamic spirituality.

It is a positive sign to see that recently, the Islamic University of Science and Technology in Kashmir created the first major university-based center of Islamic spirituality in the Islamic world, called the International Centre for Spiritual Studies. Much of Kashmir is under Indian rule and is a colony for the moment. I was invited to the opening of the center, but I could not go to Kashmir. I sent a video address, however, to be shown at the center's inauguration. The situation being what it is, I felt that it was necessary on that occasion to recall that authentic spirituality is not the same as the pseudo-spirituality à la California that is now so prevalent. That fact itself made me sad. I had to remind people in one of the great centers of both Islamic and Hindu culture in India that authentic spirituality is based on revelation and religion, on an in-depth knowledge of reality, on what is ultimately real. Why is spirituality important? Because the Spirit is important, and the Spirit is a formidable reality. It is not just a mental concept; it is part of the basic truths that Islamic metaphysics has always taught. The Quran says, *al-rūḥu min amri rabbī* (Q 17:85; The Spirit is from the Command of my Lord), implying that the Spirit is at the highest level of reality below the Divine Order Itself.

A field closely related to religious ethics and that, in a sense, embraces it—one that has become very popular especially in North America—is what is called the history of religions or comparative religion. A multiplicity of religions has always existed, but now awareness of them has gained new significance. Reference is made to the multiplicity of religions in the Quran, which, as I mentioned, speaks in many verses with an awareness of the presence of the multiplicity of religious forms. *Sūrat al-Māʾidah* refers to people who are saved as not only Muslims but also Christians, Jews, Sabaeans, and others whose names are not explicitly mentioned (Q 5:69), but the Quranic term *al-dīn* always implies the multiplicity of religions. Even the term *islām* is not limited to the religion revealed through the Quran, for Abraham, Christ, and his apostles are also called *muslims* in the Quran (see Q 3:67 and 3:52, respectively).

Now, the very reality of a multiplicity of religions is a challenge to every religion in the world today, the satisfactory response to which can be found only in esoterism and metaphysics. Such a challenge did not exist in days of old except in a few cases. Armenians were never a challenge to the Muslims of Isfahan, although they lived across the river from them. Nor were they a challenge to the Muslims of Istanbul, although Muslims would see them in the street every day. Synagogues, churches, and mosques were often in the same neighborhood; in fact, there are still a church and a mosque just two hundred yards apart in one street, where there once was also a Jewish synagogue. Although all three were on the same street, worshippers in each lived in their own closed worlds, and there was generally no need on their part to expound religious pluralism, although there were some exceptions.

Secularism combined with modern communication weaken, to a large extent, the walls and challenge the homogeneity of each religious universe. One of their consequences is the presence of other religions in our lives wherever modernism has spread. Why is it that so many young American students are very interested in other religions, and far fewer, let us say, Egyptian students hold the same interest in them? I have lectured from time to time at the University of Cairo and have observed this phenomenon firsthand. The reason for this occurrence is that most Egyptian students still live, for the most part, in the Islamic universe, despite secularization and other forces, whereas many American students live in an "open world," where even religion, including their own, is relativized. Even if they come from a southern Baptist family where they were told to pay no attention to Muslims and Buddhists, often in their very first year of college, either they become agnostic or fundamentalist or their minds open up to other religious worlds and they begin to study other religions. I have had dozens and dozens of students like this at The George Washington University, where I have been teaching for over forty years. Students come from all over the United States, and eventually many see that they have no choice but to open their minds to other religions and to take them seriously.

Here again, Islam possesses a certain advantage in that it is based on the universality of revelation and also that it encountered a multiplicity of religions within its borders and in neighboring areas before the advent of modernism. Except for European pagan religions, Western Christianity met non-Abrahamic religions only after the rise of modernism; so awareness of the multiplicity of religions and modernism in a sense went together in the Western Christian mind. In the Islamic world, however, over a thousand years ago, al-Bīrūnī wrote an extraordinary book on India, *Taḥqīq mā li'l-Hind*, in which he discussed Hinduism, Kashmiri Buddhism, and so forth. This work is, in fact, considered by many as the first scholarly book on what has now come to be known as comparative religion. Since Muslims have always known with certainty that there are other religions, they were not threatened theologically in the modern era as were Christians; Muslims did not, therefore, react existentially to the wave of comparative religion and the history of religion that began to be taught in Muslim universities. In fact, this field did not attract much attention in the Islamic world until about fifty years ago. Now, however, there are many universities in Egypt, Iran, Türkiye, Pakistan, Indonesia, Malaysia (which, by the way, has a large non-Muslim minority), and many other Islamic countries that teach various religions.

Where does Islam find the necessary philosophical and theological teachings within its own tradition for the proper discussion of other religions? This is a question that contemporary Muslims must now answer. Christians, especially in the West, are trying hard to formulate what they call the theology of religions. We Muslims have a much easier task, but that task must be based on understanding in depth our own metaphysical tradition. We do not need to discuss any sources other than the Quran and *Ḥadīth*, the traditional commentaries upon them, and sapiential writings derived from our revealed sources. These sources explain fully the metaphysical knowledge of the multiplicity of religions.

The Quran says, "And had God willed, He would have made you one community, but [He willed otherwise], that He might try you in that which He has given you. So vie with one another in good deeds" (Q 5:48). Why does God want us to vie with each other? There are many discussions on that topic in traditional commentaries and also independent works dealing with this command. Obviously, there is a profound metaphysical and theological reason for that statement. Many of our great theologians and Sufis have faced these issues, and we have a very rich tradition in Islam that speaks about this matter.

I shall conclude by mentioning an issue that has come very much to the fore in the last few years, about which Muslims have been singularly silent until quite recently. I mention it on every suitable occasion that presents itself, because I think that besides purely religious matters, the most important issue facing humanity is the question of the environmental crisis. The degradation of the environment, global warming, pollution of the land and the seas, the dying out of whole species—these disasters are all well known to us. Many people try their very best not to think about them, and the pious among us often take recourse to the truth that everything is in God's Hands. But in all honesty, we should not get up tomorrow morning, say our prayers, and then continue this destructive mode of life claiming that everything is in God's Hands in any case. The responsibility for praying has been placed upon us by God; therefore, to say that it is up to Him whether or not we pray is an absurd assertion.

It is also absurd that some Muslims think, as do some Christians, that this devastation of God's creation is all part of God's plans. Since He created the natural world, He can do with it whatever He wants, and so we should not bother with it. That is a very common although dangerous attitude that one sees in many outwardly pious Muslims as well as Jews and Christians, who by and large deny that an environmental crisis even exists. This attitude is especially strong among evangelical Christians. Among nonevangelical Christians, however, there are many who not only recognize the existence of the problem but also believe that surely God holds us responsible for it. When God said, *alastu bi-rabbikum*, we did not respond by saying, "You are our Guide; decide for us." He gave us the freedom of choice, and we must also choose how we deal with the severe man-made crisis unfolding in His creation, in the natural environment.

Needless to say, this crisis that we all face involves a very complicated set of issues. It involves economics, politics, and similar fields, but those are secondary compared to the fundamental issue of the loss of metaphysical knowledge and the sense of the sacred quality of nature as well as our responsibility toward it. The present environmental crisis involves the desacralization of nature, the turning of nature into an "it" to be plundered and raped as she has been throughout the last few centuries, first by the West and now by the rest of the world. This rape of nature is completely against the Islamic point of view, completely against the Quran, and against the teachings of other sacred scriptures. Islamic metaphysics and cosmology provide profound knowledge of causes and reasons that explain why, in fact, one should not desecrate nature, why nature is sacred, and why nature has its own norms that must be respected and followed. Rūmī has a poem that says,

کاشکی هستی زبانی داشتی
تا ز سرها پرده‌ها برداشتی

If only the world of existence had a tongue,
So that it could lift the veil from the Divine Mysteries.[7]

That verse points to the heart of Islam's philosophy of nature. For Islam, nature is always living; not only plants and animals but also the Sun and the Moon are our brothers and sisters as they were for Saint Francis of Assisi (d. 1226). How many times does the Quran mention and swear by the Sun and the Moon and other phenomena of nature, such as the pomegranate and the fig, which are tiny in comparison with the planets? Everything in nature participates in the deepest sense in the Quranic revelation; yet today, Islamic countries are among the worst polluters of the natural environment in the world. The Islamic world is doing a very good job in trying to be first in something at least—but, alas, in a negative way. As concerned Muslims, we have a duty to be critical of the current situation and to think of these matters seriously. Metaphysical knowledge and its applications are essential for the in-depth understanding of the causes of this tragedy and its solution.

Fortunately, over the last several years, even in Wahhabi-inclined Arabia, there has come into being a green movement led mostly by women rather than supposed leaders of society. In Iran, the first Muslim country where the environmental issue was addressed by myself and a few others over half a century ago, with great opposition from many quarters, we helped create the first national park system in the Islamic world. Before Syria was devastated by war, it also had a good program to preserve the natural environment. But despite bright spots here and there, overall, much of the Islamic world is in a very bad situation from an environmental point of view.

When we speak about protecting and restoring the integrity of the natural environment, our responsibility goes far beyond perfunctory recycling, beyond just throwing our trash in a can rather than in the Nile River or the Persian Gulf. Much more is needed than such actions, although they are also worthwhile on their own level. The question is how we can live in harmony with the natural environment as a sacred trust and as part of God's creation. The environment is not our servant; it is our cocreature, you might say. All creatures together constitute the life of this world. Hence the destruction of this cocreature will surely lead to the destruction of ourselves; we are committing not only ecocide but suicide by destroying the natural environment around us.

7. Rūmī, *Mathnawī*, 3:4725.

A word must be said as to why I began to speak about the environmental crisis in a serious way as a spiritual crisis before the subject gained public attention. Unlike Rachel Carson (d. 1964) in her book *Silent Spring*, which detailed specific ways in which human beings were harming the local environment, such as toxic chemicals being released into New England rivers, actions that you might say are the symptoms of the problem, in my book *Man and Nature*, I turned to the worldview that allowed the spiritual crisis that has led to the environmental crisis taking place. Why is it that the Islamic world is one of the last parts of the world to pay attention to this matter? I have written over sixty books, about fifty in the English language, nearly all of which have been translated into Persian, and others that were written originally in Persian. Yet, one of the last books of mine to be translated from English into Persian was *Man and Nature*. It should have been perhaps the first, and this is in my own country, where an environmental movement has existed for some time but not as a top consideration for the ruling authorities.

The environmental crisis is now a global phenomenon, but as soon as the value of the stock market declines, few in positions of authority speak about the environment, and they wait until the economic crisis is over. Meanwhile, we have destroyed a large part of the forests of the world and have polluted even the oceans. Also, although the crisis is a global problem, it makes no sense to remain passive and pursue our current behavior in the Islamic world and elsewhere while downplaying its significance. Islamic metaphysics provides one of the most powerful and clear images of the world of nature—what it means spiritually, what it means to our existence here on earth, and what role we have in relation to it. The legal parts of such matters are stated in the *Sharīʿah*, but the underlying intellectual and spiritual elements are stated in our metaphysical teachings. Of course, for some devout Muslims who do not feel that they need to know these reasons, who act according to the *Sharīʿah* without questioning their mode of behavior toward nature, the injunctions of the *Sharīʿah* seem to suffice. Other human beings, however, ask Why should I do this?, Why should I do that?, Why not throw dirt in the water?, Why preserve trees and forests?, Why is that little bug so important that I should not kill it?, and so forth. The answers come, in our perspective, from the integral Islamic tradition itself and, more specifically, from that part of the tradition that has to do with metaphysics. In my next and final lecture, I shall turn to the application of metaphysics to various domains, including cosmology, which concerns directly the world of nature and our role in it.

3

Some Applications of Metaphysical Principles

In this final of three lectures on metaphysics and some of its applications, I shall discuss the significance of metaphysics for the knowledge of religion as well as art, science, and certain other aspects of human activity pertaining to the act of creating. I have touched on a number of these issues in the previous lectures, but I shall return to some of them here in greater detail. The first two lectures dealt primarily with principles and how to gain access to them, and while they also dealt with some applications, this final lecture will concentrate mostly on how to understand and evaluate the contemporary scene in light of metaphysical and traditional principles.

What I have tried to impress upon the listener thus far is that there is a body of knowledge called metaphysics and that metaphysics is a supreme science, a sacred science, *scientia sacra*, that deals, on the one hand, with the Ultimate Principle, with the Root (*aṣl*)—that is, with God, with the One who is the Source of all things—and, on the other hand, with the manifested order in relation to the One. It should be repeated here that the meaning of the word *science* has become very limited in the English language, more so than in French, because in English it pertains usually to only a particular form of knowledge called science—that is, a quantitative study of the realm of nature and mathematics. When I use the term *science*, however, I am using it in the original meaning of the word, which is "organized knowledge." In this sense, metaphysics is defined as a body of knowledge or science concerned with the Principle of Reality and Its manifestations in relation to the Principle. This body of knowledge is attainable only if we have the necessary capability to understand it; that is, there has to be a relationship or adequation between the knower and the Known, without which the knower cannot know the Known.

In order to know metaphysics, we have to search deeply within ourselves; we have to reach that faculty—that is, the heart-intellect—within us that will enable us to understand first principles and their applications. In the same way that if we had no eyes we could not see the external world physically and if we had no ears we could not hear sounds, so too we have to have the appropriate faculty that is able to perceive this knowledge. This faculty is associated traditionally with the heart and the eye at its center. The heart is much more than the organ in our breast. In addition to the physical heart that is on the left side of our breast, we have a spiritual heart that resonates at the center of our chest. Although it is not sensed by most of us in our everyday lives, it can sometimes manifest itself even physically through physiological reverberations or other sensations—a phenomenon into which I shall not go now. It is that heart-center that is able to know reality in the sense that I am speaking about here. The Quran associates emphatically real knowledge with the heart, not with the brain. Throughout the Quran, it is the heart that knows, not the head. Needless to say, it is not mental knowledge but principial knowledge that is associated with the heart. That is where the Intellect as I defined it in my previous lecture is located. That is where the eye that is able "to see" the Divine Reality is found. Although the *ʿayn al-qalb*, the "eye of the heart," is closed for most of us, still there is the possibility for us "to see" this Reality if we dedicate ourselves to opening that inner eye.

With the hope that you now have some understanding of this body of metaphysical knowledge, I shall now discuss why such knowledge is so important for the underpinning of everyday human life while emphasizing again what I mentioned earlier—namely, that while it is not necessary for everyone in a human society to have this kind of knowledge, it *is* necessary for some to have it. For example, it is not necessary for everyone in, let us say Toronto, to be an electrical engineer, but if there were to be no electrical engineers in Toronto, the lights would not work in this auditorium. Society as a whole—in our case, a healthy Islamic society—always needs a few who have knowledge of principles. Islam was able to educate throughout fourteen centuries of its history a body of men and women who *knew* in the real sense, who knew principles contained in this form of supreme knowledge and who were also able to apply them as circumstances required. We are perhaps the first generation in the whole history of Islam for whom this knowledge has become eclipsed—not totally, thank God, but to such an extent that many of our people, especially the younger generation, are totally unaware of its existence. At the same time there is a whole movement within the Islamic world to try, in fact, to neglect and forget about this knowledge, as if God has sent his Prophet only for externalities and not for the purpose of gaining knowledge of God Who is the Origin, the Source, and the raison d'être—that is, the reason for the existence of religion itself.

Let us turn again to the significance of metaphysics, first of all for religion itself. I mentioned this point previously, but now I want to give some concrete examples. Let me start with the example that has been dealt with thousands of times in Western literature and has caused millions of people to leave the Christian Church in modern times, and that is the question, Why, if God is good, is there evil in the world? I am sure all of you have faced this question: Why is there evil? The question of evil has been dealt with in Western writings all the way from philosophical texts to literature such as *Crime and Punishment* by Dostoyevsky (d. 1881); it is one of the favorite themes in Western thought. It might appear as a great paradox that, in contrast to the West, few if any Muslims, Hindus, or Shintoists have left their religion because they could not answer this question, while I have known personally hundreds of educated Westerners who were Christians but who have left Christianity because they could not answer it. This itself is a paradox. Why is this so? Why is this question not such a major issue in Muslim Egypt or Hindu India or Buddhist Thailand? Why does no one leave Buddhism because there is so much poverty in Myanmar? This is a profound and pertinent question that cannot be avoided.

The answer to this question cannot come simply from the external teachings of religions that say that God is good and that we should also be good while acknowledging that there is evil in the world, even though the world is created by the Divine. The question of theodicy thus arises. Thousands of metaphysicians and theologians in nearly every religion have addressed it, and a religion that does not have a proper response to such a cardinal and central subject will lose some of its followers; they are going to seek elsewhere for an answer. The best example of this phenomenon happening can be found in the open book of the history of Christianity in the West. Anyone who studies the history of Western Christianity knows why it is that so many of the intelligent Europeans in modern times have left the Catholic Church: It was over this very issue, about which much has been written over and over again. Now, metaphysics and it alone has the ultimate answer to this query, an answer that is not understood by everyone, but it is there for those who can comprehend it. Their having understood it will prevent this draining away, this loss of the lifeblood of the religion that happens when there is no one in a religion who understands this issue and is able to provide the necessary metaphysical answer to this question.

An answer can be provided very quickly, although for some, it may take a lifetime to understand it. The response may be summarized as follows: We start with the certainty that only God is the Absolute, the Infinite, and Perfect Goodness. Being Infinite, He must contain within Himself all possibilities; otherwise, He would not be Infinite. Since His Infinity of necessity includes all possibilities, it also includes the possibility of negating Itself, and that possibility is the world. To say *world*, *manifestation*, or *creation* means to speak of separation from God—the Supreme Good and the only Absolute Good—and it is that separation that is the source of all that we call evil. That is the essential explanation, very simply put, but to understand it, one has to understand the relative in light of the Absolute, to comprehend levels of reality, levels of being, and ontological hierarchy, and it is this understanding itself that has been lost in secular philosophy in the modern world. Even faithful people usually see existence in terms of a simple division where there is God and there is the world, including us. The fact that there *are* levels of being has been lost philosophically if not in religious practice, while this truth is foundational to Islamic as well as other forms of traditional metaphysics, including the Christian.

This basic truth was gradually lost in modern Europe and was finally replaced by the theory of evolution; that is, the vertical ladder of reality, which extends from the lowest to the highest reality until it finally reaches God, became horizontalized and temporalized and the metaphysical explanation of evil forgotten. Instead of man progressing vertically to the angelic world and ultimately to the Divine Reality Itself, evolutionary theory tells us that we have ascended from apes and that we shall evolve, at least according to some evolutionists, to a point where we shall be capable of doing practically anything we want—including building ugly, polluted cities—before turning into supermen and becoming "gods" on earth. Evil is seen as anything that impedes that process of progress. Of course, some may say that I am making a parody of evolution, but what I am seeking to bring out here is that it is one of the greatest absurdities forced upon humanity, with dire consequences for our relation to the world of the Spirit as well as to the natural world itself.

This kind of secularization and horizontalization of the vertical hierarchy, which was foundational to all metaphysics, has, however, become very common these days. The reason why Islam, for example, did not have the crisis that Christianity faced in the nineteenth century when Darwinism came into being was because the vertical hierarchy had not disappeared there as it had in the modern West. The fact that Darwinism hardly caused a ripple in the Islamic world—or in other traditional worlds, for that matter—religiously or philosophically, is quite interesting. At that time, it was not even a major intellectual issue, except for a few people of peripheral importance who talked about it. With the spread of modernism into traditional worlds, however, evolution began to gain some popularity in Hindu India and also, to some extent, elsewhere in the East, including the Islamic world, but there have been no Islamic Sri Aurobindos among Muslims in the nineteenth and early twentieth centuries. Now, however, Muslim defenders of evolution are also appearing. For example, one author working out of the United Arab Emirates has been writing recently on evolution from an "Islamic" perspective, and one of his books was even endorsed by some well-known Muslim writers in the West.

The reason that there is this radical difference between the influence of evolution in the West and in the Islamic world is that the awareness of the vertical hierarchy was and is still very much alive in Islam.[1] And it is by means of knowledge of this vertical hierarchy that we remain aware of the derivation and also separation of the levels of existence from that which is the Source of the hierarchy. Traditional metaphysics teaches us that only God is good and also that God has to create, since Creator is one of His revealed Names. It also teaches that He is Infinite, implying, in a sense, the necessity of the "separation" from the Absolute, which constitutes the domain of relativity that is the world. Furthermore, this elongation and separation is what appears to us as evil. Dante said so beautifully that evil and Hell are separation from God. In the Quran also, the pain of Hell is shown to be even greater than man envisages because in the infernal states, man has awareness of God but is separated from Him, and this separation is much worse than if one were not to see Him and be conscious of the gift of proximity to Him. Simply put, this existential separation from the Good is the origin of evil.

Now, the statements I have made will not be found in a book of *fiqh*, of Islamic Law, or even ordinary books of *kalām*. These statements come from metaphysical principles that I have tried to simplify in a few sentences. However, a religion that does not have an intellectual answer to such questions is going to lose its most intelligent people and will become a religion of simply blind followers who do not concern themselves with the inner meaning of its teachings and who do not think about these matters. The Quran encourages Muslims to think when it uses such terms as *yatafakkarūn*, *yafqahūn*, and *yaʿqilūn*. All these terms are verbs that are found in the Quran concerning the different forms of correct thinking and intellection in which we should engage. So, we certainly should not be among those who stop thinking and

1. For a metaphysical as well as scientific and paleontological critique of evolutionary theory, see Seyyed Hossein Nasr, *Knowledge and the Sacred* (Albany: State University of New York Press, 1989), 221–52.

using our *ʿaql* and believe that a good servant of God accepts everything on blind faith alone, because doing so goes against the teachings of the Quran itself. Faith in the truth of religion is essential, but so is the correct use of *ʿaql*.

Then there is the question of the nature of our soul and, in fact, our whole existence. As I asked earlier, Where do we come from? Why are we here? What is our end? Any pensive person will ask such questions. The Quran itself summarizes the answer in the majestic verse *innā li'Llāhi wa-innā ilayhi rājiʿūn* (Q 2:156; Truly we are God's, and unto Him we return), the verse Muslims often recite when someone dies. When we think about it deeply, however, we realize that it is metaphysics that provides us with the most profound significance of this verse that so many people recite without understanding all its layers of meaning. "Truly we are God's" means that we come from Him, and that in turn means that God has created us from a pre-existential archetype that is contained in the Divine Intellect, in the Divine Reality, and is then existentiated by that Reality. Therefore, we have a preexistent reality in God; otherwise, we could not have said before the creation of terrestrial man *balā shahidnā* (Yea) to God when He asked the progeny of Adam, *alastu bi-rabbikum, qālū balā shahidnā* (Am I not your Lord?) and they answered, "Yea, we bear witness." The complete translation of the verse is as follows: "And when thy Lord took from the Children of Adam, from their loins, their progeny and made them bear witness concerning themselves, 'Am I not your Lord?,' they said, 'Yea, we bear witness'—lest you should say on the Day of Resurrection, 'Truly of this we were heedless'" (Q 7:172). Since this covenant was made with God before Adam and his progeny were existentiated on earth, it means that we had a preterrestrial Adamic reality "in God" or "with God." In order to understand this covenant fully, one has to understand metaphysics because it took place beyond time, beyond history, beyond our earthly reality and mental existence. The covenant belongs to another order of reality beyond the physical and mental, and that reality is the concern of metaphysics.

After asking where we come from, the question arises: Where are we going? We find the most obvious answers in the eschatologies described in the Quran, the Bible, or other sacred scriptures, but these characterizations also have an esoteric and sapiential meaning. From beginning to end, the Quran emphasizes the importance of eschatology. From *Sūrat al-Baqarah* to almost the end of the Quran, the Sacred Text comes back again and again to the themes of Heaven and Hell, felicitous states and states of suffering, and so forth. The levels of existence are, however, more complicated than just two states of the paradisal and the infernal, and there are many Islamic sources that mention, for example, the *darajāt*—that is, grades and degrees of Paradise, Purgatory, and Hell. What do they imply? The answer to the question is not to be found in simplified eschatology; it involves understanding the states of being. It is related to the knowledge of how and why there is Divine Mercy that encompasses all things: *wa raḥmatī wasiʿat kulla shayʾ* (Q 7:156; My Mercy encompasses all things). How is it that this Mercy can, in fact, go beyond God's own teachings about punishment and reward? How does Divine Mercy work? The deepest answers to such elements of religion are not usually to be found in ordinary ethical and legal aspects of religion; these are matters to which only the inner metaphysical aspect of religion has always responded and is still capable of doing so. Therefore, if one takes that inner aspect out of a religion, it will become atrophied and crumble. It can no longer provide answers to some of the most important questions that perceptive human beings ask.

Take even something as simple as this question: Why should I be good? Almost all of us face this question in daily life. We also see good people suffering and evil people having very comfortable lives, and we wonder what is going on. Where is God's Justice? Either we do not concern ourselves with this disparity and just cling to our faith, saying, "I shall not ask this question; only God knows; He is the Wise [*Ḥakīm*]," or we try to delve more deeply into the matter. And if we do delve more deeply into it, we come back to the long chain of cause and effect in human life, to what the Hindus call karma. This word has entered into the English language now, and it means ultimately cause and effect considered not only morally but also cosmologically and metaphysically. Every cause has its effect. Every good thing we do has its positive effect; every evil thing we do has its negative effect, and this chain goes back even to our preterrestrial and postterrestrial existence. We come into this world not as a book of blank pages; rather, we come with a certain heritage and nature. You might say that there is already a book written about our state of being to which we add in our lives. This doctrine is not mentioned as much in the exoteric dimensions of the Abrahamic religions as it is in the Indian religions. Why is it that some children are very intelligent while some children are not? Why is it that some children can swim well while others cannot do so even if they try to learn? Why is it that some are good athletes and others are not? Why do some learn languages well or are artistically inclined and others do not and are not? Some will ponder these questions and even ask where God's Justice is. If such a person cannot answer these questions satisfactorily, the foundation of his or her faith becomes shaken gradually; again, the deepest answers are metaphysical.

We must understand, therefore, that authentic metaphysics is not a luxury but a necessity. It is foundational for the survival of integral religion, a fact that cannot be overemphasized. One can give many other examples of questions for which intellectually and religiously inclined people seek answers, such as these: Why is there a world? And why *this* world? These are profound issues for which a fully alive religious collectivity has to provide answers, although as mentioned before, not everyone in that collectivity seeks those answers or feels in need of them. The grandeur of a religion such as Islam is that it was able to create a system whereby answers to questions of the deepest kind were not available only to the intellectual and spiritual elite but percolated through the whole of society, and thus different types of people could gain at least some understanding of principles and their applications, even if not on the highest level, but according to their needs.

One can find answers to the most profound questions in traditional Islamic texts, all the way from abstract and difficult metaphysical books that take years to understand fully, to those of greater accessibility such as are found in wisdom literature and poetry. I can bear witness to the fact that in Iran, it would take years to study a text of metaphysics and/or Islamic philosophy with traditional masters. Sometimes it would take three weeks to study just one page, not because of linguistic difficulties in the Arabic or Persian text, but because the depth of the meaning it contained could be fully understood only gradually. There was always an inner meaning expressed in a few words that needed extensive explanations to comprehend. Such texts are not meant for everyone, but they are there for those who need them. Furthermore, as explained earlier, when the outstanding Persian traditional teachers such as ʿAllāmah Qazwīnī (d. 1975), who was one of the greatest metaphysicians of his day, used to teach in a school in the bazaar of Tehran, even some of the beet-sellers in the bazaar would come and sit in his class. Islamic education was open to everyone; a person did not have to register and pay tuition and do all these things that modern education requires. The students ranged from philosophically advanced *mulla*s and *ʿulamā'* to the shopkeeper interested in philosophy and gnosis.

Moreover, in the traditional Islamic world, education was always free for everybody; people could simply go to a *madrasah* mosque such as al-Azhar to study. In fact, that is how it was at al-Azhar until just a few years ago, but now they have made regulations like a modern university and do not let everyone in anymore. In the *madrasah*s, a person would sit down and listen to the teachings of a master, and he would derive benefit from it according to his capacity to understand. The teaching was based on a gradation of knowledge, and these various levels of knowledge had a way of seeping into various classes of citizens throughout society. Just as coffee percolates until the whole liquid becomes coffee, these very exalted teachings would gradually percolate to some degree into the ordinary consciousness of people, some of whom had little formal education. Of course, some masters also taught classes, especially in metaphysics, that were open only to advanced and well-trained students.

In the domain of the transmission of spiritual knowledge, Islamic literature played a very important role, especially poetry. I cannot overemphasize this fact; it is something the likes of which we do not have in the West. The only countries that could be considered exceptions, to some extent, are Spain, because of the Islamic influence on it, and Italy, where some (though not most) people know at least a few verses of Dante's *Divine Comedy* by heart, and the sapiential poetry of this work is widely available and a living reality there even today.

As a Persian, I can attest to the fact that in Iran, there is almost no one, no matter what his or her educational level is, who does not know at least a few poems of Ḥāfiẓ (d. ca. 792/1390), Saʿdī, and Rūmī by heart. Such was also the case until recently in Muslim India and Pakistan. These poems contain the most exalted metaphysics but also speak to those interested in the spiritual life and the meaning of existence in general. I often recount the following episode to my students, an event that is very telling. It happened that one evening I was outside of Lahore, where I had gone to visit the beautiful tomb of Mīyān Mīr (d. 1045/1635), the great Qādirī saint of the seventeenth century. At that time, the tomb was surrounded by fields; now, unfortunately, the slums of Lahore have encompassed it. When I came out of the tomb, it was about eight o'clock at night, and there was no transportation available except one tonga, the small, horse-drawn carriage that they still have in Pakistan and India. The driver's clothing showed that he was a very poor man, and he asked me in Urdu, "Where are you going?" I know very little Urdu, but I understand many simple phrases because of the similarities of Urdu to my mother tongue, Persian. I answered in Persian, saying, "I am going back to Lahore." He said, "Get in." I was surprised that he understood me. It took us about forty-five minutes to get to town. During those forty-five minutes, he recited incessantly classical Persian poetry, mostly of Ḥāfiẓ and Rūmī. He expounded more authentic metaphysics in those forty-five minutes than I had learned in any classroom at Harvard, where I had taken courses with some of the greatest teachers of medieval philosophy in the West.

That tonga driver was still a product of traditional Islamic civilization; that is, he was living in a world where something of metaphysical knowledge, through poetry especially but also through other forms of art, percolated into the prevailing common culture. This transmission occurred not only through traditional poetry but also through music, the plastic arts, architecture, and so forth; all the traditional arts communicate this principial knowledge on various levels and by different means throughout traditional society.

So it is that Islam produced the means whereby this very exalted science of metaphysics—which, in itself, is only for the few—could, in a sense, permeate through the whole structure of society and become a protective code that served to prevent the rebellion of many minds against the Divine as happened in the West after the Middle Ages. That rebellion has now penetrated the minds of many young people in the modern world, including even some parts of the Islamic world.

Why is it that so many parents have trouble these days with their teenage children over the question of religion and ethics? They are rebelling, but many parents do not have the means to overcome the doubts of the new generation. If we were living in older days in the Islamic world, there would always be means available to respond to our children's questions, but those means have now been lost to a large extent in the modernized sectors of even the non-Western world, not to speak of the West itself.

I shall conclude this section by repeating that there is no way for a religion to survive without it providing answers to certain inner questions that are of a metaphysical nature. Once those questions are no longer answered, what happened in the West to religion will happen to other religions, including Islam. There are no exceptions. Any human being who is honest with himself or herself must accept the truth that to be honest with God, one has to be honest with oneself. One must face the fact that he or she has fallen into a state of doubt if that is indeed the case.

In the Islamic world, we have the supreme example of this honesty in al-Ghazzālī, the great Shāfiʿī *faqīh* and theologian who, at the peak of his academic career, fell into doubt and who then left everything—his family, his position, his wealth—and disappeared for ten years in order to regain certitude. Young people who are honest with themselves, once they fall into a state of doubt, either will hide their doubt and thus become hypocrites because they fear their parents or the society around them or will stop being seriously interested in religion and become lukewarm toward it. They may possibly even turn against religion and start looking elsewhere for answers, often hiding the inner crisis within their souls. I have known many students from an Islamic background who have left the world of faith because they have had certain questions that neither the ambience around them, nor the imam in the mosque, nor their parents could answer satisfactorily. So, the first role of metaphysics is the preservation of tradition, at whose heart stands religion.

The Muslim intelligentsia must always keep in mind the history of Western Christianity from the fifteenth and sixteenth centuries to today.

Although France was called the bride of the Christian Church and the British monarch is the head of the Anglican Church, according to recent studies, there are more Muslims in France and England who attend the Friday prayers than there are Christians in those countries who attend Sunday Mass, despite Muslims being a minority population. Just think for a moment about this fact; let us not gloss over it. Why has this phenomenon taken place? Let me try to provide some of the deeper reasons. It is not my intention here to analyze step-by-step what happened from the fourteenth century in the nominalist movement in the Middle Ages, or what happened in the Renaissance and later, or why metaphysics was eclipsed in the West. Such detailed analyses can be found elsewhere in the seminal works of Guénon and Schuon as well as in my own humble writings, but in any case, the net result is what we see before our eyes. What we are witnessing should be the best proof of the significance of metaphysics, not as a luxury but as a necessity, like the heart that we never see but whose beating is essential to our lives. We see our hands, we see our eyes, we see our ears, but we do not see our heart, even though it is the most important part of the body and the organ that governs everything else. Metaphysics is like that; it is essential inner knowledge not discernible to the outward eye, yet it is an ever-present reality.

* * *

We must now delve more fully into this question: How does this supreme science, whose significance I have tried to reiterate, apply to fields other than religion? As mentioned in the first lecture, one of the great tragedies that occurred in the West resulted from the time of Aristotle in considering the supreme science of metaphysics as a part of rational philosophy, whereas in fact, the truth is the other way around. Authentic philosophy is an application of metaphysics to certain domains of knowledge, which we call "philosophical knowledge." So, the priority comes not with philosophy but with metaphysics understood traditionally. Authentic Islamic philosophy, or what is called *ḥikmah* in Arabic, begins with metaphysics, as mentioned so succinctly by Suhrawardī (d. 587/1191), while even Peripatetic (*mashshāʾī*) works end and do not begin with it in contrast to works on gnosis that are metaphysical throughout and where *philosophia prima* remains *prima*. For example, *al-Asfār al-arbaʿah* (*The Four Journeys*) of Mullā Ṣadrā begins with metaphysics, Ibn Sīnā's *Kitāb al-shifāʾ* (*The Book of Healing*) begins with logic and ends with metaphysics, while the *Fuṣūṣ al-ḥikam* (*The Ringstones of Wisdom*) of Ibn ʿArabī is metaphysical from beginning to end. The root of real knowledge resides in *ilāhiyyāt*. Later Islamic philosophy, which is usually more metaphysical, begins with the supreme science and then turns to other forms of knowledge in light of this primal knowledge. As for Suhrawardī's great book *Ḥikmat al-ishrāq* (*The Theosophy of the Orient of Light*), it opens with logic—but a logic that is related in its foundation to illumination and not just ratiocination.

In Islam the first important application of metaphysics to fields other than religion occurred in philosophy, which has survived to this day because the later schools of *ḥikmah* have always been rooted in metaphysics and are, in fact, its application to various philosophical matters. Later Islamic philosophy has applied metaphysics to the realm of philosophy, including even logic. Today, in modern thought logic is pitted against metaphysics, and even some famous Western philosophers such as Bertrand Russell have written books and articles on logic as opposed to mysticism and metaphysics. We should ask ourselves the question, "If we say two and two is four, then logically, four and four is eight. But where does that certitude come from?" Why are we so certain? We can simply say, "Oh, this is logical." Do not forget, however, that the word *logic* is related to the term *logos*, which in Greek means both "knowledge" and the "Word of God" that corresponds and is related to *kalāmu'Llāh* (which is, in fact, a name of the Quran) and also *ʿilmu'Llāh* in Arabic. The word *nāmūs* also entered into Arabic from the Greek *nomos*, but since it is a rarer term whose philosophical meaning only experts know, I will not turn to it here.

The root word that we employ in English now (from *logi*, *logia*) is used for many forms of knowledge—geology, theology, psychology, and so on—as well as in the word *logic*, which, as I mentioned, has to do with the Word of God (Logos) in the traditional perspective. How this term was translated into Arabic is of some interest. The word *logic*—that is, the science of logic—was translated into Arabic as *manṭiq*. Originally it was translated as *manṭūq*, in *bāb al-mafʿūl* or the passive form from the root *n.ṭ.q*, which means "speech" or "word," thus preserving the original Greek meaning of *logos*. *Manṭiq* here has nothing to do with creaturely speech, which is one meaning of the word outside of this present context. Rather, here it has to do with *nuṭq* in the original metaphysical sense of the term as the Divine Word, the Word of God that also has to do with logic, even though logic in modern thought is considered as being opposed to religion, to mystery, to mysticism, and to metaphysics.

We can pose the question: From where does the certitude of logic come? The answer is to be found in metaphysics. This certitude comes from the reflection of the Intellect upon the mental plane. It is a knowledge contained already in the Intellect; we do not usually even bother to ask about this phenomenon because we think that we understand it already. As long as we have a little sense of logic, we understand what it is. A child begins to understand logic early in life as this Intellect becomes more and more reflected on the mental plane of his or her being. If that reflection were not to be there, human beings in whom it would be lacking could not be logical. This truth holds because logic is not an innate faculty of the mind itself but a reflection of another faculty that is above the mind. The reflection of the Intellect is not always the same in all people. Some people are very logical, some people are somewhat logical, some people are not logical at all, and so forth.

It is interesting to note here that when we have a serious argument, many of us, both men and women, become emotional. Those of you who, like me, have had experience in this matter for many decades will bear me out. What happens is like water that is stirred up by the wind: The reflection on the water is lost, but as soon as the water becomes calm again, the reflection comes back. We all experience such moments in our own lives.

Therefore, to understand why there is even such a reality called logic, why it is that it works in so many cases in life, and why its conclusions correspond to external reality, it is necessary to have metaphysical knowledge; otherwise, these questions remain mysteries. Why is it that I can build something externally on the basis of what I conceived in my mind with the result that it can possess objective reality, just as I conceived it? What is the link between the logic in my mind and that machine working out there in that factory and producing what it is producing? The answer comes down, essentially, to applied metaphysics and whether it is correctly understood or rejected. This rejection is why, today, these questions are seldom asked and why most people do not concern themselves with such things. Why is it that in my mind I know that if my bicycle tire deflates, I have to find a way to pump it up and fill it with air again? How and why is there a relation of cause and effect between the thought in my mind and the external object that is the bicycle? How is the subject related to the object and how is there correspondence between them?

With all the theories and studies of modern philosophy, psychology, and other disciplines, there is, as yet, no fully satisfactory answer to the question of the relation between subject and object in modern thought. That is why there are so many prevalent theories. What creates this correspondence between subject and object? As is well known, modern philosophy is not fully successful in its response to this question. It has usually sought to reduce either the subject to the object or the object to the subject, ending with an untenable "monism"—and if not that, then with an unexplainable dualism. These days in the West, it reduces the subject mostly to the object with the resultant materialism, saying that there is no such thing as the mind as an independent substance—that the mind is an epiphenomenon, a biological phenomenon of physical brain cells and neurons—and that it is nothing more than the functioning of those cells in the brain that constitutes what is called the mind. Then there are the few idealists in the history of Western thought, such as George Berkeley (d. 1753) and others, who say that, in fact, there is no external world independent of the mind, and they also have some defenders today even among certain brain specialists. One can also point to the remarkable English neurologist Sir John Eccles (d. 1997), who won the Nobel Prize in Medicine for his books, especially *The Self and Its Brain*, cowritten with Karl Popper (d. 1994), and *How the Self Controls Its Brain*, which have sought to prove that the mind is not an epiphenomenon of the brain; rather, the brain is an instrument the mind uses.[2]

To understand truly and explain in depth this relationality is a very difficult matter if one limits oneself to the prevalent modern scientific point of view, based as it is on Cartesian bifurcation, and so most people take the prevailing scientific view for granted. Let us say, for example, that I call out to my son and he responds, "Yes." What is really involved here? The frequency and amplitude of the sound or light waves that come out of my mouth and face can be measured, but what about the message that is conveyed by the sound and light? Why is it that he hears it or sees me and knows that it is he whom I am addressing and also understands my message? What is taking place here? If we rely solely on modern science, we cannot answer that question in a completely satisfactory manner.

Metaphysics, however, *is* able to provide the answer, and that answer lies in the correspondences that exist between various levels of reality on both the vertical and horizontal planes; these are the ontological correspondences that exist between us as human beings and the world about us. Let me give you another example from another order of the deep levels of relationality involved by asking the question: Why is it that modern human beings are the only living creatures on earth who can destroy the terrestrial natural order? All the really big animals—elephants, whales, dinosaurs—are or were much bigger than us. Human beings are quite small when compared to many of the big creatures on earth, yet we are the only ones capable of destroying the earth's balance and, therefore, destroying not only the animals' habitat but also our own. Nobody can provide an answer to that question if man is considered only as an evolved monkey, the result of the process of life on earth. Evolutionary theory posits that *Homo sapiens* evolved from apes; yet

2. Karl Popper and John C. Eccles, *The Self and Its Brain: An Argument for Interactionism* (New York: Routledge, 1983); John C. Eccles, *How the Self Controls Its Brain* (New York: Springer, 1994).

why is it that the apes were not able to cause such destruction of nature as we can? What happened in the so-called evolutionary process to bring about the possibility of the destruction of the biological forces that created the evolutionary process itself? Prevalent scientific responses to such questions cannot be taken seriously, and so these difficult questions are rarely discussed and are usually glossed over in ordinary scientific texts. They are, however, profound questions, the surface of which I have only just scratched. They are questions that traditional metaphysics and cosmology alone can answer intellectually.

Now, let us go one step further and continue with an issue mentioned briefly earlier. One of the greatest dangers that the world faces today is its domination by modern science and its applications that consider the world to be independent of God or any spiritual reality. Of course, there are some modern scientists who believe in God, but such belief is a private matter for most of them. As I mentioned, the "God hypothesis," or vertical causality, is irrelevant to the prevalent hypotheses of quantum mechanics as well as to relativity or even to the classical physics of Newton, as the works of the physicist and mathematician Wolfgang Smith have shown. It is worth mentioning here that Professor Smith argues that a lack of attention to vertical causality is the reason that the current theories of quantum mechanics are unintelligible on the philosophical plane.

Whether or not an individual science student, professor, or practicing scientist believes in God has no relevance to the science with which he or she is concerned. Modern science has declared its independence from the Divine Reality. In the name of freedom of thought, it declared its independence from religion and also from metaphysics. In the seventeenth century, as E. A. Burtt (d. 1989) showed in his classical book *The Metaphysical Foundations of Modern Science*, there were still attempts made to find a metaphysical foundation for physics.[3] Kepler, Newton, and Leibnitz as well were interested in this issue, but serious interest in theological issues in relation to science was given up, save for a few exceptions. The result is that in the modern West, science is totally separated intellectually from both religion and metaphysics. People live today in the most antimetaphysical age of human history, and many who still have faith have a compartmentalized mental life.

In the influential Vienna Circle of the early twentieth century, which led to the logical positivism that has dominated so much of American philosophy today, metaphysics has been talked about as if it were a pattern of cobwebs.

3. E. A. Burtt, *The Metaphysical Foundations of Modern Science* (New York: Harcourt, Brace, 1925).

Positivism considered metaphysics to be a relic from an earlier age before science advanced, and therefore, metaphysics and gnosis had to be removed from the intellectual arena completely. As a reaction to this antimetaphysical atmosphere in the West, there arose serious interest not only in *Existenzphilosophie* and certain forms of phenomenology but also in non-Western traditions. Later there appeared also the phenomenon of the New Age, with its "metaphysical bookshops" full of literature dealing with "spirituality" as well as the mystical aspects of nature, both usually diluted and cut off from tradition. Although much that is presented by this phenomenon is not serious metaphysics, still it shows the deep need of many for a kind of knowledge other than the prevalent scientistic one. To the extent that it can, this movement runs counter to the official knowledge that dominates Western society, a society that is rooted in a secularized science that, to all extents and purposes, is "worshipped" by many people. Even for many Muslims, when it comes to knowledge of the world, it is not Allah but science that is "god"—that is, the ultimate authority. Scientism is very prevalent among such Muslims, and they are totally enthralled by science and its applications in technology, not only for economic reasons, but primarily for the dominance and power it bestows on those who possess and control it.

Modern science itself, if absolutized and not taken as *a* science of nature but as *the* only acceptable science of nature, becomes one of the greatest dangers for humanity. If it were relegated to the legitimate domain that is in accordance with its nature, that would be fine, but that is not the case. Its absolutization and the negative effects of its applications are now being felt everywhere in the world, as one sees in the environmental crisis.

A coinventor of the gas laser in 1960 was a Persian Muslim physicist at MIT, Professor Ali Javan (d. 2016). He was bitterly disappointed to see his invention, whose initial purpose was to advance cutting and welding techniques in industry, put to use as a military weapon to burn and kill hundreds of people from the air. I knew him personally and know that the first time this military use occurred, he became very saddened and talked about the tragedy that ensued, saying he had created a monster. There are many other such examples of the unintended applications of apparently benign inventions and the distress these uses have caused their inventors. Another example is the case of J. Robert Oppenheimer (d. 1967), who died in grief because he had directed the making of the atomic bomb. He was a man of conscience and soon realized what a disaster he had brought about for humanity.

That example is perhaps an extreme one, but even worse than the extreme example of the instant death of many is the slow death that we are all suffering through the application of modern science resulting in the destruction of the natural environment. It is said that if a frog were to be thrown into a pot of boiling water, it would jump out immediately and save itself, but if it were put into a pot of cold water and the temperature of the water were turned up slowly, the frog would not become aware of the increasing danger it was in, and it would soon die from the gradual rise of the temperature of the water. What is true in the case of the frog *is* happening to us and our planet now—that slow and not-always-perceptible "burning up" of the biosphere. If climate change were to happen suddenly, like a huge fire encompassing our whole environment, one that everyone could see (although in recent years, it has now almost reached that kind of fever pitch in a few places), we would all be out in the streets to force an end to the practices causing such destruction. But since the process is a slow death, few people are fully aware of it; most people just go about their business as usual and do not pay sufficient attention to this crucial matter.

Now, there is no way to be able to criticize in depth the underlying reasons for the misdeeds and the inherent limitations of modern science and technology except through the traditional understanding of metaphysics and cosmology. There are some critiques, and a number of them are quite cogent and pertinent. There are some methodological criticisms—it is a field in which I am also involved and so I am aware of them—but most such criticisms do not really touch the heart of the matter.

At the heart of the matter lie these questions: What is the nature of reality? What kind of science, what kind of knowledge about the nature of reality do we obtain with the particular methods that we are using? Does the method we are using exhaust the totality of the reality of the subject we are studying? How does the truncated vision of man and nature propounded by modern science and its applications affect the natural environment and our relationship with it? If you are studying the forest only from the point of view of its timber and how much income you will receive in the market by selling the wood from the trees that are cut, you are missing out on the life of the birds that live in the trees of the forest and the other creatures that live underneath the trees. We limit our understanding of the web of life in this way all the time, and it is only metaphysics that can really perform the service of penetrating the heart of the reality that is involved. It is a great tragedy that criticism of these matters is not heeded sufficiently and that those few people who do make such criticisms are often ignored. I have been in this battle for over half a century and speak from long experience.

* * *

Let us now turn to another crucial and central discipline: the science of man, anthropology, but not in the modern sense of the term. Anthropology comes from the Greek word *anthrōpos*, meaning "the human being," *insān* in Arabic, or "man" in the original English sense encompassing both male and female. Since *logos* means "study," *anthropology* means "the study of the *anthrōpos*." I usually do not favor the use of the word *anthropology*, because today the anthropology that is taught in colleges rarely deals with the total nature of man as *anthrōpos*. It deals often with how many silk blouses women buy in London and what relation that has to their income or what the dietary habits are in a certain village in Nepal or the size of the craniums of the people there, but *anthrōpos* in the spiritual and metaphysical sense is rarely discussed.

More recently, postmodern theories combined with opposition to "essentialism" have also become dominant in the academic study of the field. I have known some students who have studied anthropology but became dissatisfied because they found that they could not deal with what they were seeking, the study of the *anthrōpos* understood traditionally, but instead had to deal with man as either a biological creature, economic animal, or social animal—merely a creature formed by a culture severed from transcendence. The students could not get into deeper issues of what it really means to be human even when studying cultural anthropology, not to talk about physical anthropology. Let us use the term for the moment, however, as meaning "the science of man"—literally, anthropology without its modern limitations. Then one could say that one of the most important roles of metaphysics is making possible a traditional science of man, which includes both traditional psychology and anthropology.

Let us then start with psychology. In order to know something, you have to comprehend—that is, embrace it; this is what *comprehend* means in English. In order to comprehend something, you have to embrace it. As I said in the first lecture, the Latin verb *comprehendere* means "to embrace" in the sense that if I were to meet a dear friend, I would embrace him; this is the etymological meaning of *comprehendere*. The Quran says, *wa kāna'Llāhu bi-kulli shay'in muḥīṭ^{an}* (Q 4:126; God encompasses all things), which also means that He comprehends all things. *Al-Muḥīṭ*, the All-Encompassing, is one of the Divine Names. Whatever exists, God has an *iḥāṭah* over it—that is, He encircles it, embraces it in "His Arms," you might say. Of course, these terms are to be understood not anthropomorphically but symbolically. To repeat: In order to know something, you have to comprehend it. That truth means that only the greater can know the lesser. We can know, for example, the nature of the wood of the chair we are sitting on, because we belong to a higher level of reality than the wood, and our minds can, therefore, understand it. Modern psychology tries to understand the psyche of a human subject through the psyche of another person who is called a psychologist in the modern sense. This situation is unacceptable in Islam and other traditions such as Hinduism. Only the person who knows the Spirit can come to know the psyche in depth and treat it. Therefore, to know who we really are is a crucial matter for psychology and also anthropology, which are sciences, along with biology, of the realities that constitute the human being.

The Quran contains a fully developed anthropology, the science of who we are. First of all, we were created by God. God blew His Spirit into us: *nafakhtu fīhi min rūḥī* (Q 15:29; I Breathed into him of My Spirit). So, our spirit comes from the very Spirit of God, and the Spirit of God is therefore in us. Then He has endowed us with many different powers. I am putting aside here all the descriptions that the Quran gives of the stages of gestation of the child in the womb of the mother; I am speaking not about those miraculous events, incredible as they are, but rather about the net result—that is, the birth of a being who contains multiple levels of reality within himself or herself, who is both free and invited by God to submit his or her freedom to Him. This is the paradox of being human. God has created us with free will, but we are called servants of God—that is, those who surrender themselves to Him. God wants us to submit our free will freely to Him; so He creates a being who has free will, who has an array of different faculties, including "vertical" faculties—emotional, mental, intellectual, and spiritual—that cannot be seen outwardly but the totality of which, along with bodily faculties, comprise the traditional understanding of what constitutes a human being.

The Quran, moreover, discusses at length both *al-insān*—that is, men *and* women—as well as men and women separately as distinct beings complementing each other. It addresses the whole question of gender and topics related to the differences and similarities of the two genders created by God. I shall not go into that matter now, but I would like to point out that this division of human beings into male and female should be understood also metaphysically and cosmologically and not only biologically and psychologically. Why does God say He created everything *azwājan* (Q 78:8; in pairs)? God is God; why could He not create without pairs since He has infinite Power, for He is *'alā kulli shay'in qadīr* (Q 2:284; Powerful over all things)? It is one of those questions to which one responds either by saying, "Well, I do not know. God says it is so; therefore, I am not going to ask," or by pondering what the meaning of it is. Again, the answer comes back to metaphysical and theological knowledge that insists at the same time that He created us in pairs and that the Principle or God is One. Creation means separation from the One, and separation means, first of all, complementarity, just as the first separation from the number one is the number two (*azwāj*[an]), after which comes the multiplicity of numbers.

In the traditional world, there are different formulations of the science of anthropology that take account of the whole of the human being in every way and deal with all the vertical as well as horizontal faculties that he or she has, along with the differences between the genders and why these differences exist. Islam insists on the equality of men and women before God ethically and eschatologically as well as on the lack of equality but complementarity between them in this world. The gates of Heaven, Purgatory, and Hell are open or closed equally for men and women. There is no discrimination from that point of view, but the social and familial obligations, the economic division of inheritance, and so forth show a kind of division of labor and responsibility, you might say, in Islamic society, where the man is responsible for all the expenses of his wife; even if she be a millionaire, she does not have to spend a penny for family expenses if she does not want to do so. The reason why, according to the *Sharīʿah*, sons inherit twice as much as daughters is because of the responsibility placed on the male to take care of the female, of his mother, children, aunts, daughters-in-law, and so forth, if need be. There is a kind of "equality" created through what appears to be a lack of "equality," something that some Muslims themselves do not understand. As a result, people oftentimes think of themselves as wiser than God, including those in the Muslim feminist movement; but we are not wiser than God.

To understand why, traditionally, the divisions between the genders are as they are, again, one needs to look at the matter as a metaphysical and cosmological issue and not only a biological, social, or legal one. To understand gender, to understand the sexes, to understand sexuality itself, one must see their deep metaphysical basis. Human sexuality is not just a biological animal act; it has to do with the complementarity of the inner psychological and, to some extent, mental nature of the sexes and why, in fact, the male and female attract each other. These are really wondrous mysteries of creation that are often glossed over, but they are matters that sages over the ages have explained in profound ways.

* * *

Let us now return for the sake of emphasis to the important subject of art, with which I dealt previously. Those of you who know my writings know that I have been concerned with the question of Islamic and, more generally, traditional art for over fifty years. In addition to my writings on the topic, I have succeeded in helping save many of the most beautiful artistic monuments of Iran from being destroyed and facilitated the preservation and revival of many traditional arts. It is a strange paradox and also a great tragedy that although in the Islamic world, not everything in this domain has been destroyed, the process of destruction continues in many places, while in the West, almost everything that could be destroyed was already destroyed some time ago, and what remains is now protected and preserved very well. There is no chance of Notre Dame in Paris being torn down, as are many traditional mosques that then have monstrosities built in their place. There is no chance that the beautiful old walled city of Carcassonne in southern France or the historic buildings in Bath in England and other such sites will be destroyed now, whereas in the Islamic world, we see right before our eyes the destruction of some of our great architectural heritage every day.

The Tehran where I was born has changed greatly in my own lifetime—all of its gates are gone, most of its gardens are gone, and much of the beautiful architecture that we had, including my own beautiful traditional Persian house, are all gone. So we are living through a constant tragedy of the loss of the beauty of our living space. Look at what happened to Cairo. I am not Egyptian, but when I was twelve years old and on my way to America for the first time, I spent over a month in Cairo and visited an area that was called "Garden City"; it was like a spacious, lush garden even if it were part of the modern quarter of the city. Now, you find much of the greenery destroyed. In the Cairo in which there are still to be found numerous masterpieces of Islamic architecture, some of the ugliest buildings in the world were built by the Soviets during the time of Gamal Abdel Nasser. It is astonishing to see such ugliness in the city in which were built Fatimid, Ayyubid, and Mamluk buildings, such as al-Azhar University, the Sayyidunā al-Ḥusayn Mosque, and the Ibn Ṭūlūn Mosque, just to cite a few outstanding examples. The contrast is unbelievable.

As mentioned already, throughout my adult life, I have been involved in these matters, not only in writing as a philosopher and Islamicist, but also in practical ways. When I lived in Iran, I brought the Egyptian architect Hassan Fathy, known for his work to revive in Egypt the use of adobe and traditional mud construction as opposed to Western building materials and methods, to Isfahan when, with the help of Empress Farah, we organized in that city the first international conference ever held on Islamic architecture. I arranged for the University of Chicago to publish Hassan Fathy's book *Architecture for the Poor*, but although it was a masterpiece, it was completely ignored in Egypt at the time it was written in the 1960s.[4] Now, however, it has become

4. Hassan Fathy, *Architecture for the Poor: An Experiment in Rural Egypt* (Chicago: University of Chicago Press, 1973).

fashionable among wealthy Egyptians to build in the Hassan Fathy style for their weekend homes outside Cairo. I have also been involved with the repair of the Shalimar Gardens under the direction of the president of Pakistan at the time, because I felt a sense of responsibility to help preserve the beautiful art of the Islamic world, and I have always been deeply touched by it in all its forms because of its spiritual and metaphysical content. Perhaps I should mention that I am a person who loves the classical music of the Islamic world and had the fortune of being brought up surrounded by the purest classical forms of Persian music. The great Persian maestro Abu'l-Hasan Saba (d. 1957), who visited our house often, was my father's cousin, and I was surrounded by a very rich artistic tradition that has always remained deep in my heart.

One cannot talk about metaphysics in depth without art. In fact, to be able to expound metaphysical teachings clearly and correctly is itself an art. Remember that in Islam, metaphysics percolated to society at large oftentimes through poetry and music, but not only through them. Every traditional work of architecture in the Islamic world is an application of metaphysical principles and of traditional cosmology, which is derived from metaphysics.

Concerning cosmology, which is a complicated matter into which I shall not go at length here, it needs to be remembered that the word *cosmology* means "knowledge of the cosmos" and that *kosmos* in Greek means both "order" and "beauty." These days, however, cosmology has come to have two completely different meanings: one the traditional and the other called modern cosmology, which is really an extension of modern physics. The laws of physics that are discovered and then tested in laboratories are now extended ad infinitum to the whole of the cosmos, and this field is then called cosmology, which changes every few years. It has given us the Big Bang theory, then accordion theory, then string theory. I do not even bother to read about each new theory anymore.

I gave a lecture a few years ago in Seattle to the American Academy for the Advancement of Science on traditional cosmology in contrast to modern cosmology. Some of the world's most famous cosmologists in the modern sense were there, but they wanted, nevertheless, to hear about traditional cosmology, which, as I have already said, is the application of metaphysics to the realm of relative existence, to the cosmos; that is, it is the science of knowing the cosmos in light of metaphysical principles. In this context I might add that it was in 1964 that Harvard University Press published my book *An Introduction to Islamic Cosmological Doctrines*.[5] Unfortunately, nothing

5. Seyyed Hossein Nasr, *An Introduction to Islamic Cosmological Doctrines* (Cambridge, MA: Harvard University Press, 1964).

has superseded it in all these years; I wish some work had done so. It is still in print and is still the only easily available book on the principles of Islamic cosmology that people who are interested in the topic can read. I should add that there is a fine book by Osman Bakar (*Qur'anic Pictures of the Cosmos: The Scriptural Foundation of Islamic Cosmology*) that is available easily, but it is not an introduction to the topic as is my book.[6] In the intervening almost sixty years, there should have been at least ten books better than mine written on the subject. In any case, in this book and subsequent writings, I have tried to bring back to life what real traditional Islamic cosmology is, and I have written much on this subject in later years.

I do not want to get into an in-depth discussion of this subject here because it is a technical field of its own, but I do want to emphasize that traditional cosmology is a science of the relative in light of the Absolute. It is an application of metaphysical principles to the domain of relativity, and it depicts the cosmos as an icon. An icon of Christ in Christianity or of Krishna in Hinduism is a painting on one level, but it speaks of something beyond itself, and that is what traditional cosmology is; it is like sacred art, like sacred painting, and these domains go very much together. It is essential to understand that the principles of cosmology deal with how the cosmos really works in light of spiritual principles, not only in its physical aspects taken as an independent reality.

Traditional cosmology is also inseparable from traditional arts and architecture, and through its application of metaphysical principles, metaphysical truths penetrate into the arts. Traditional buildings are based on symbolism and cosmology; they are, in a sense, manifestations of metaphysical principles in stone and brick or other materials used in different arts. From the Sultan Ḥasan and Ibn Ṭūlūn Mosques in Cairo to the Sultan Aḥmad Mosque in Istanbul to the al-Qarawiyyin Mosque in Fez to the Great Mosque of Kairouan in Tunisia to the remarkable mosques in my own country, such as the Jāmiʿ Mosque of Isfahan to the Bādshāhī Mosque of Lahore and so many more, these buildings are created as a means of taking us to a reality beyond ourselves, to providing a space in which the Divine Word reverberates, because the space of the mosque is *defined* by the reverberation of the Divine Word. What could be more metaphysical than that? I am, of course, not speaking here about the bland and often ugly modern buildings that are called "mosques." I am speaking about traditional mosques or even traditional houses of worship of other orthodox religions for that matter. In the same way that the Islamic

6. Osman Bakar, *Qur'anic Pictures of the Cosmos: The Scriptural Foundation of Islamic Cosmology* (Selangor: Islamic Book Trust, 2016).

world has among the most polluted cities on the planet, we are also catching up with some modern countries in creating some of the ugliest places of worship. This phenomenon is a real tragedy because Islam is based on beauty. There was no ugly mosque before the twentieth century. From the beautiful mud structures in sub-Saharan Africa, which are based on the same principles as the Bādshāhī Mosque of Lahore or the Shāh Mosque of Isfahan, although their appearances are strikingly different, all the way to the ornate faïence (tiled) mosques of Iran, Afghanistan, and Uzbekistan, all the architecture of the Islamic world was imbued with beauty.

In the premodern period in the Islamic world, even the vernacular architecture and the architecture of private houses and their inner gardens and so forth were all applications of the same principles that were involved in the building of traditional mosques. The late Titus Burckhardt has brought out these principles clearly in his masterly book *Art of Islam: Language and Meaning*, which I recommend highly to every Muslim who is interested in his or her civilization.[7] In that book, he explains clearly the metaphysical principles and the symbolism that are involved in Islamic art. We cannot understand symbolism without understanding metaphysics, because symbolism reveals levels of reality; it shows us the reflection of a higher level of reality on a lower level. Why do Christians kiss the cross? They do not do so because it is two pieces of metal or wood stuck together; they do so because it symbolizes Christ. Christ is not that wood; he belongs to a higher order of reality, but his being is symbolically related to the physical cross. Every symbol contains levels of reality and opens unto a reality beyond itself.

Sadly, in the modern West, the symbolist spirit has been lost. Traditional civilizations existed in a world in which the symbolist spirit was fully alive, in which nearly everything made was symbolic, and therefore, the art of those civilizations was always combined with symbolism. Furthermore, the in-depth meaning of symbolism can be understood only metaphysically because metaphysics is the key to the understanding of the ontological basis of symbolism. It is not accidental that as soon as authentic metaphysics disappeared from the mainstream of Western culture, symbolic art also nearly disappeared from the West.

Yes, there were movements such as the Symbolistes in France in the nineteenth century, a movement that was led by Paul Verlaine (d. 1896), Charles Baudelaire (d. 1867), Stéphane Mallarmé (d. 1898), and others who tried to revive symbolism, but without having any deep knowledge of it and its

7. Titus Burckhardt, *Art of Islam: Language and Meaning* (Bloomington, IN: World Wisdom, 2009).

metaphysical foundation. A much more effective attempt to revive symbolism in the West occurred in the twentieth century in the hands of several thinkers and scholars and most of all by traditionalists such as Guénon and Ananda Coomaraswamy (d. 1947) followed by Schuon, Burckhardt, Martin Lings (d. 2005), and a certain number of Catholic artists in Britain and elsewhere who were also devoted to oriental metaphysics. Those in the circle of Coomaraswamy and other traditional masters, even those who were Catholics, studied the Upanishads and the Quran. Their movement spread to the United States, especially the Northeast, with the result being that for a while, there was a revival of traditional Latin calligraphy, Christian sacred art, and symbolism itself, and greater attention began to be paid to the iconic art of the Orthodox Church that has continued to have a vibrant life.

One of the significant trends in scholarship in this field during the last several decades can be found in the works of Mircea Eliade (d. 1986) and his school, which had its roots in works of traditional writers who first wrote in the modern period about symbolism in the deepest metaphysical sense. Guénon's book *Le symbolisme de la croix* (*The Symbolism of the Cross*) brought an awareness of symbolism to Europe and America among at least some Western people, but in traditional civilizations such as the Islamic, the symbolist spirit remained very much alive and was not eclipsed.[8] When a civilization such as the Islamic accepts the development of schools of thought such as the modern or the so-called puritanical reformist movements for whom the word *symbolism* has no metaphysical meaning and reality and for whom everything is only literal, that development sounds the death knell of traditional art right then and there.

The survival and use of symbolism, however, guarantees the continuity of sacred and traditional art. The beautiful mosques built along the corniche of Jeddah were built not by Saudi architects but by one of Hassan Fathy's best Egyptian students, the aforementioned Abdel-Wahed El-Wakil, who was also indirectly one of my students, a man for whom Islamic symbolism is alive and real, a man whose life's work has been dedicated to resuscitating it. The rebuilt Qiblatayn Mosque and other remarkable new mosques in Arabia were all designed by him and one or two others who were also of the school of Hassan Fathy.

So, one of the very important applications of metaphysics is to be found in the use of symbolism in art, through which traditional art functions as a means of bringing us back to the Divine through ordinary forms that

8. René Guénon, *The Symbolism of the Cross*, trans. Angus Macnab (Hillsdale: Sophia Perennis, 2001).

encompass us in our earthly life; that is the basic role of traditional art. One cannot enter a classical traditional Islamic mosque without thinking of the sacred. Unfortunately, now as people enter the Kaʿbah precinct, too many of them are glued to their cell phones and overwhelmed by the hundred-story buildings now surrounding the House of God. The sacred nature of the space has been destroyed along with much of the Islamic art that surrounded and adorned the Kaʿbah.

* * *

My last words on the arts turn to perhaps the most interiorizing of all arts: music. Do not think that all music is *ḥarām* because some jurists have said so. Even Ayatollah Khomeini (d. 1989) said that only music that is lascivious and leads one to sin is *ḥarām*, or forbidden, by Divine Law; otherwise, music in its totality is not *ḥarām*. He made this statement in the most important *fatwā* or religious edict ever given by one of the most powerful *fuqahā'* in Islamic history on music, and his *fatwā* caused classical Persian music to be performed again on Iranian radio and television as well as in concerts. Many *ʿulamā'* concurred that not all music is *ḥarām* but only certain types of music that dissipate the soul. What Islam did was to interiorize music. It did not develop "social music" but did permit music for weddings and funerals, military marches, music in relation to the crafts as well as folk music, not to speak of Sufi music, which remains prevalent throughout the Islamic world. It should also be remembered that the chanting of the Quran is the highest form of music in Islam, although it is not called music.

This interiorization of music is seen especially in the role it plays in Sufi practices. The greatest performers of Islamic music of Northern India—Bismillah Khan (d. 2006), Ali Akbar Khan (d. 2009), and others—came from Sufi families, without exception. I knew many of them personally; they were men of the Spirit. In Iran, most of our great musicians until the last generation either belonged to Sufi families or were members of Sufi orders. In Tehran, when my father used to take me to the tomb of Ṣafī ʿAlī Shāh (d. 1316/1899), the great saint of the nineteenth century, I would see many Persian musicians sitting there. The same is true for Arabic music. It was Sufism that always kept classical Arabic as well as other forms of traditional Islamic music alive. In the Ottoman world, it was especially one single Sufi order, that of Mawlānā Jalāl al-Dīn Rūmī, the Mawlawiyyah Order, that preserved and passed on classical Turkish music. If you turn on the radio in Istanbul to a station that plays classical Turkish music, it is usually music performed by Mawlawīs that you will hear. There are movements now to revive traditional music in Türkiye for the larger public, but generally speaking, it is the music of the Sufi orders that alone has carried out this task throughout the years since the secularization of the country. Traditional Ottoman music, like other traditional music throughout the Islamic world, is rooted in interiorized Sufi music. A similar situation exists elsewhere as far as the relation between Sufism and music is concerned.

In addition, in the Islamic world, there is music for special occasions that also can be considered traditional and that the Prophet himself allowed specifically on occasions such as weddings and other joyous celebrations, funerals, journeys of caravans, or going into battle. Furthermore, traditional music of various guilds and agricultural activities allowed by the *Sharīʿah* was developed throughout Islamic history. These occasions and activities employed the power of different kinds of traditional music "to set the tone" for the activity taking place. Military music, for example, was loud, bracing, and often fast-paced, while that to accompany bricklaying was steady and monotonous. In any case, traditional music in all of its forms had and still possesses a spiritual aspect—and in the case of Sufi music, a metaphysical one.

Now, however, in many places, we are experiencing a tragic secularization of music not just in the lyrics sung but even more so in the melodies themselves. Just as traditional architecture was destroyed by removing its symbolism and metaphysical foundation, the preponderance of Western pop music has had a devastating effect on the life of traditional music in many Islamic lands. It is the exact same phenomenon we see everywhere. We are confronted with the loss of traditional art's metaphysical and cosmological foundations. The popularity of what could be called musical "junk food" usually involves fame and wealth for those musicians who succeed in this genre, and this fact has now become true in many places all over the world; Muslims are no more guilty of indulging in this "sin" than Indians, Japanese, or anybody else. When musicians stop playing traditional music, parents stop encouraging their children to learn it, instrument makers stop making traditional instruments, and the music withers away and gradually dies. It is like the extinction of a species, and it is happening all over the world where traditional instruments, their makers, and their players have been cast aside in the popular culture, although, thank God, the tradition has still survived and has even been revived here and there.

As a person who has much interest in and a little knowledge of traditional music, I can say that this phenomenon is not confined to the Islamic world alone. There are great Hindu authorities who are just as critical of what some Hindu musicians are doing to the *rāga*s and other forms of classical Hindu music, and the same is true in other places such as Japan, where those who are purists with regard to Japanese music are very critical of much that is being done in the Japanese musical world. This phenomenon is global. Tragically, the bastardization of so much of the world's artistic heritage is widespread, to say the least. I need not use stronger language.

What is the cure for this trend? It is the metaphysical understanding of the nature of reality and the role that art plays as a complement to thought that brings metaphysics into our lives. If you were a peasant or a cook in the traditional Islamic world and were working in the field or in the kitchen during the day, you would hear someone chanting the Quran or someone singing vocational chants, and it is quite likely that you too would be among them. The fact that traditional music can make some metaphysical and cosmological truths enter our consciousness is related to the spiritual character of traditional music. The spirituality experienced through music belongs to another realm that is distinct from such Sharīʿite injunctions as making ablutions or eating *ḥalāl* meat; these two levels must not be confused with one another. Traditional music nourishes the spirit, and it is to be found in different forms everywhere. Wherever Islam went, it either created or transformed the existing traditional art, not just any art, into a traditional Islamic spiritual art. One of the best examples of this phenomenon is found in North Indian music. Hindu India is the land of one of the greatest civilizations in the creation of traditional music, but North Indian music owes much, if not most, of its later existence to Muslims. It is not accidental that one of the greatest masters of North Indian music was the nawab (the Muslim equivalent of maharaja) of Rampur, Reza Ali Khan (d. 1966). He collected and put into contemporary form modes of North Indian music. His students or those influenced by him included such famous musicians as Ravi Shankar (d. 2012), Ali Akbar Khan, Vilayat Khan (d. 2004), and even Bismillah Khan.

I shall conclude my comments on music with a personal account that demonstrates how profound the importance of metaphysics is to music. Because of my intense love for music, I have passed many nights in India from sunset until almost sunrise just listening to *qawwālī* music in Sufi centers or to other types of classical Indian music in other places. Once we invited Bismillah Khan to Tehran. He played the shehnai (*shāhnay*), a beautiful oboe-like instrument whose name Bismillah Khan considered to be derived from the name Ibn Sīnā but is probably derived from the words *shāh* and *nay*; that is, "the royal flute." I had gone to the Tehran airport myself with a driver to fetch him and his sons who were accompanying him. I told him that we had rooms reserved for them in Tehran, but he said, "I am not going to the city." He was speaking Urdu and I was speaking Persian, but we could make out what the other was saying. He said, "No, no. I first want to go to Mashhad for pilgrimage [*ziyārat*]." Mashhad is one of the most holy cities in Iran, where

ʿAlī al-Riḍā, the eighth Shiʿite imam, is buried and where numerous pilgrims, including many Sunnis, go on pilgrimage. I said, "All right; I shall arrange it," and I got a ticket for him right there to fly to Mashhad. Although the plane was about to take off, I asked the pilot to hold it so Bismillah Khan could get on. (Yes, those were the good old days when I could do such things.)

He said to me, "Dr. Nasr, there are only two things for me in life: *sāz wa namāz*." Those of you who know Urdu understand that in that language, *sāz* can be used to mean a musical instrument in general, although it is the name of a particular instrument in Turkish and Urdu. However, *sāz* can refer to any musical instrument, such as a kamancheh, tar, or sitar, among others. Of course, *namāz* means "canonical prayer." This one phrase of his—*sāz wa namāz*—summarizes perfectly what I am trying to express to you now: The great musical art that is one of our treasured heritages was, from the very beginning, wed to the inner dimension of religion, to metaphysics and cosmology. How much is being lost today, especially among the younger generation, who harm their own souls by listening to cacophony rather than real music from morning to night!

Namāz here does not only mean an ordinary canonical prayer; it also implies more generally the prayer that draws us to the Divine. One is reminded here of the famous verse of Bābā Ṭāhir (d. 401/1010): *Khushā ānānki dāʾim dar namāzand* (How joyous are those who are always in the state of prayer). On that level, *namāz* implies more than the obligatory prayers, and it was to this meaning of *namāz* that Bismillah Khan was referring. Repeating with the lips *Allāhu akbar, Allāhu akbar* but thinking meanwhile about what you are going to sell in the bazaar later is not really *namāz* in its full sense. To be a truly great musician, one must achieve the interiorization of prayer, the inner *namāz*, which can then be expressed through the *sāz*. I hope that this story will remain etched in your memories as an example of how significant in our civilization metaphysics and spirituality always were. Spirituality is the practical aspect of metaphysics; metaphysics is doctrinal knowledge of the Real and the world of manifestation as manifestation of the Real, *al-Ḥaqq*.

QUESTIONS AND ANSWERS

Question-and-answer sessions followed only the first and third lectures, since the third lecture was delivered nearly immediately after the second. Although in the first session, attendees posed their questions orally, in the second session, their questions were written out due to a technical issue.

Questioner 1: In the context of metaphysics, how do we understand the Quranic verse (Q 50:16) that says that Allah is closer to us than our jugular vein?

Seyyed Hossein Nasr: What a good question. Metaphysics asserts that God is the Center of the circle of reality, and that Center is everywhere and nowhere. Wherever something *is*, there is God. On purpose, I am using the verb *is* without a complement. What I mean is that where there is being, where something exists, God is present because He is the Center of all existence, the Source of all being, and in fact, the only Being. The Quran brings out this truth majestically by saying that He is closer to us than our jugular vein—that is, the vein in our neck where we feel our heartbeat if we put our finger on it. So, God is closer to us than our heartbeat. It is the jugular vein that brings blood into the brain and, therefore, makes our life possible. God is closer to us than life itself. Why? Because we exist. To exist is to exist in the circle of existence, the circle at the Center of which is God. And let us remember that there is no circle without a center. It has been said that modernism constitutes a circle without a center, metaphorically speaking. This metaphor describes so much of modern life. It is as if we are living now in a circle whose center we have lost. Of course, to do so is impossible in reality, because to say *circle* means to have a figure with a center, and this beautiful verse of the Quran is an allusion to that truth.

Questioner 2: What is your advice for students who would seek to challenge Western secularism in the classroom, especially when reading the likes of Marx (d. 1883) or Žižek (b. 1949), without succumbing to defensive methods of argumentation? In other words, how does one respond intelligently when one has not been exposed to years of the aforementioned technical training?[9]

SHN: I sympathize with you very much. I am also a liberal arts teacher at a university; of course, in my classes, we do not have this problem, but I understand you. First of all, do not argue with the teacher and just keep your mouth shut until you get an "A" and end the course successfully. Seriously, that is my advice. Secondly, do not get into an argumentative mode in a class where the teacher does not even want to consider your view. Also, for those of you who are in college dormitories and other social settings where students get together and have long discussions

9. This question was signed, "A frustrated humanities major at a liberal arts college."

deep into the night, I advise you not to argue about religious matters with people who are opposed to the religious perspective, because they might drag your psyche down a kind of sliding slope until you find yourself in a state of doubt and do not know where you stand. This is the advice given by al-Ghazzālī in *al-Munqidh min al-ḍalāl* (*The Delivery from Error*) It is not that you should never argue, because sometimes you are forced to do so. If you are in class and somebody asks you "What did Marx say?" you have to know and give an appropriate response. It does not mean that you have to agree with Marx; a lot of people have criticized his views.

What you do need is a certain amount of self-assurance when embarking upon such discussions. It is that quality that is often lacking among many of our students. Those from certain Muslim-majority countries find themselves in classes with students who belong to a civilization that has nuclear bombs and goes to the moon, and they know that they belong to a civilization that cannot do or make such things. It is this sense of power imbalance that creates an inferiority complex in many Muslim students, and that is a problem. The first time I was strong enough, at the age of nineteen, to stand up to my teachers at MIT, who were among the world's greatest scientists, and challenge their view of modern physics was one of the most difficult days of my life. But had I not done that, I would not be sitting here before you as who I am. You need to be strong enough intellectually and morally to be able, if your point of view is attacked, to defend yourself not in an offensive way but in a defensive way, remembering *lakum dīnukum wa liya dīn*, as the Quran says, "Unto you your religion, and unto me my religion" (Q 109:6). This *sūrah* belongs to the Makkan period, a time of opposition to the early Islamic community. Repeat this verse inwardly to yourself and say outwardly, "This is your own belief. You keep your belief to yourself, and I shall keep my belief to myself." This is different from the case of a teacher arguing that this particular student does not understand what Marx said on page 372 of *Das Kapital*, and the student has little choice but to accept what the teacher says about it. Textually, the teacher would be right even if the context of the text itself is false.

I am giving advice here as a person who has taught for over sixty years at universities all over the world and has some experience in this matter. Do not, however, take everything that you are forced to read as being the truth. Today, the Western humanities are, for the most part, based on a perspective that relativizes everything. In the way that Western philosophy is usually taught, each philosophy nullifies what came before it. This philosopher said such and such. The next philosopher said the opposite of it. Another philosopher said the opposite of what the latter said, and so on, with the assumption that there are, in fact, no permanent truths but only a temporal development of ideas. In contrast to this way of looking at the matter, I have spent years teaching Islamic philosophy based on the view that traditional philosophical teachings are related to each other creatively; they do not necessarily nullify each other. This is the traditional process in which a Suhrawardī brings a new vision and yet integrates the older teachings of Ibn Sīnā into his philosophy and a Mullā Ṣadrā does the same vis-à-vis both Ibn Sīnā and Suhrawardī.

Now, if you have to study the modern humanities, keep in mind that they are not the traditional humanities. Yes, you should try to learn some history, some English, some other languages, some literature, and if you have to do so, take courses on philosophy, but view all of them in light of traditional teachings. It is good to know something about Western philosophy, but not to adopt the modern and postmodern views of philosophy while losing sight of perennial and traditional philosophy. It is like saying that it is good to know something about Toronto traffic or the traffic in whichever city you live but not to make the traffic your main concern in life even if you get stuck in it. I am not, of course, trying to criticize Toronto traffic. Tehran traffic is even worse. But you should not be in a state of passive defensiveness. Have the certitude that God is on your side as you go through this trial. Try to do your best. Say some prayers inwardly and continue to repeat appropriate verses of the Quran to yourself.

Questioner 3: Metaphysically, how does one come to understand that which we perceive as not beautiful—for example, the ugliness of injustice—while recognizing that everything perceived is a manifestation of Allah's Attributes?

SHN: This is another way of posing the question "Why is there evil in the world?" Or it is to say, "Why is there ugliness in the world if everything is created by God? God is Beautiful, so why did He create ugly things?" To be sure, this is a very important question, but this is not really the place for me to answer this very complicated matter with the detailed exposition that it deserves. But let me just summarize the issue for you. First of all, as I have mentioned already, in Arabic, Persian, and many other Islamic languages, the word for "beauty" and "goodness" is the same: *ḥusn*. Therefore, to ask "How is it that God is Beautiful but He created ugly things?" is the same as asking "How is it that God is Good but there is evil, *qubḥ*?"

Qabīḥ in Arabic means both "ugly" and "evil" or "bad." So, the two go together in the Muslim mind and Islamic civilization and are not separate from each other.

Now, there are many answers that have been given to what you intend in your question. Islam rejects the idea that beauty is in the eye of the beholder. That is metaphysically absurd. Beauty is an ontological aspect of any thing, just like its weight is an aspect of it, although the perception of the quality of its beauty is such that each person appraises it subjectively. The reason why God allows this subjective appraisal is that through His Infinite Mercy, He has created infinite forms of beauty and has given us the freedom and capacity to appreciate certain forms of beauty and not others. There are many people in this room who appreciate very much beautiful music, but some do not; some appreciate beautiful paintings. Some appreciate neither; they appreciate the beauty of nature. Some appreciate none of these three, but they do appreciate a beautiful human face. Through this diversity of God's creation and through His Mercy, He has allowed us to develop an appreciation for certain, if not all, forms of beauty. That is why what appears beautiful to one person might not appear beautiful to another, but that does not mean that beauty is not an objective reality and is only "in the eyes of the beholder." This is one argument that can be made in response to what lies at the heart of your query. It is a matter of the perception and appreciation of beauty by each beholder according to his or her nature and propensity, not that that beauty is only subjective. Beauty, if perceived correctly, is an objective reality.

Moreover, even taking the diverse capacities that human beings have into consideration, let me pose this question to you: Can you think of the natural world, not created by human beings, as being ugly? Here we are in Canada, one of the most beautiful countries in the world in terms of nature. Some are doing a fast job of destroying its natural environment, but they have not succeeded; it is such a vast country, with beautiful forests and mountains. As soon as you get out of Toronto, everything is beautiful until you get to the next city. And this is true of most cities all over the world, not only in Canada, which I cite only as an example. There is overwhelming beauty in God's creation to be seen everywhere, from equatorial forests to the frozen landscapes near the North Pole. Can you think of something ugly in God's creation? You might say, "Oh, a snake," for example, but that is because you are afraid of it, but snakes are also beautiful in their own way. That is why people pay $400 to buy a pair of shoes made of their skin; many women who are afraid of snakes buy handbags made of snakeskin. Also consider the remarkable beauty of a spider's web.

Usually, termites and such insects do not show their beauty to us because they are too small; so we do not think about them as displaying any beauty. Now that we have microscopes, however, we can see the remarkable structures that these small creatures have and how they share in the beauty of creation. Everything that our eye can perceive in nature, from Mount Everest to a butterfly, displays some form of beauty. There is no ugliness in the world that surrounds us except in what we create, although we are also capable of creating works of beauty. Both are our specialty. The ugliness that we see on earth is the creation of us human beings. And that comes back to the fact that God has given us the freedom to reject Him.

You may ask why He has given us such freedom. The answer is that He loves us, and love has no meaning unless it is based on free will. If you coerce a man or a woman to love you, what kind of love is that? It is not real love, for real love requires free will. The famous *ḥadīth qudsī* where God says, "I loved to be known, and therefore I created creation so that I would be known," reminds us of the central significance of love. That God loved to be known means also that He had to give us the free will to love Him in order to know Him. This is a very important metaphysical issue. We should realize that we have been allowed to squander, to waste this free will that we have been given in order to respond properly to God's love to be known as creatures whom He loves, as the Quran also asserts.

Traditional man, because he still loves God, creates predominantly beautiful things. The creation of ugliness was left mostly for secularized and forgetful modern man. These are strong words, but look at the reality of the matter. If you had gone to a Native American village in the American Southwest until fairly recently, you would have seen that the objects produced there had an element of beauty even though the inhabitants were poor materially. Poverty combined with ugliness is mostly a modern phenomenon.

Why is it that so much of what we produce today is ugly even though we know it is ugly? Some people might answer by saying that these things have to be ugly because what is important is practical utility and economic feasibility, but the separation of utility from beauty is the invention of modernism, and so much the better it is for us to realize it.

So yes, we cannot stop accepting that beauty is one of the Attributes of God, as is Justice. But in the same way that there is injustice in the world because of the separation of fallen man from God, and that injustice is possible only through human agency, so is there the possibility of the creation of ugliness that surrounds us on so many levels today. You cannot say that elephants are unjust in tearing down trees and eating them. Just as injustice is a human trait, ugliness is also our invention, in a sense. One of the best proofs for the existence of God is the overwhelming beauty of His creation. People who are "nature worshippers" and who consider themselves to be atheists are not really against religion or divinity. They find God in the beauty of nature because they could not find Him in the church where they were supposed to go to experience His Presence.

The presence of beauty in nature is something overwhelming. Years ago, we had no notion of what was in the depths of the oceans. Now we have all seen photographs of coral reefs and deep-sea creatures. The experience of the incredibly beautiful combination of hues and geometric forms in the life of creatures that were hidden from us previously was saved for this age of humanity as a blessing when we have lost so much beauty in the ordinary world surrounding us. Our ancestors never saw that hidden world, but now that you can see it, just look at how beautiful it is, at how much beauty exists in God's creation. There is really no aspect of creation that does not reflect God's Beauty in some way.

So yes, to answer your question, we perceive things as not beautiful because we create things in the forgetfulness of God. All traditional art was created with the remembrance of God, and that is why there is no ugly traditional art. There is hardly any vase from a thousand years ago that is not beautiful unless belonging to a decaying or decadent culture. These are truths that cannot be denied.

My time is up. May God always be with you. May the blessings of the Prophet always be with you. Seek knowledge unto the grave, but a knowledge that will transform you and that will wound your soul and make you better human beings, *in shā 'a'Llāh. Al-salāmu 'alaykum.*

Bibliography

Bakar, Osman. *Qur'anic Pictures of the Cosmos: The Scriptural Foundation of Islamic Cosmology*. Selangor: Islamic Book Trust, 2016.

Burckhardt, Titus. *Art of Islam: Language and Meaning*. Bloomington, IN: World Wisdom, 2009.

Burckhardt, Titus. *The Essential Titus Burckhardt: Reflections on Sacred Art, Faiths, and Civilizations*. Edited by William Stoddart. Bloomington, IN: World Wisdom, 2003.

Burtt, E. A. *The Metaphysical Foundations of Modern Science*. New York: Harcourt, Brace, 1925.

Coomaraswamy, Ananda. *Metaphysics*. Edited by Roger Lipsey. Princeton, NJ: Princeton University Press, 1977.

Eccles, John C. *How the Self Controls Its Brain*. New York: Springer, 1994.

Fakhry, Majid. *Islamic Occasionalism and Its Critique by Averroës and Aquinas*. New York: Routledge, 2008.

Fathy, Hassan. *Architecture for the Poor: An Experiment in Rural Egypt*. Chicago: University of Chicago Press, 1973.

Guénon, René. *The Essential René Guénon: Metaphysics, Tradition, and the Crisis of Modernity*. Edited by John Herlihy. Bloomington, IN: World Wisdom, 2009.

Guénon, René. "Oriental Metaphysics." In *Light from the East: Eastern Wisdom for the Modern West*, edited by Harry Oldmeadow, 8–22. Bloomington, IN: World Wisdom, 2007.

Guénon, René. *The Symbolism of the Cross*. Translated by Angus Macnab. Hillsdale: Sophia Perennis, 2001.

Ibn ʿArabī. *The Wisdom of the Prophets*. Partial translation from Arabic to French with notes by Titus Burckhardt; translation from French to English by Angela Culme-Seymour. Gloucestershire: Beshara, 1975.

Lings, Martin. *The Essential Martin Lings*. Edited by Reza Shah-Kazemi. Bloomington, IN: World Wisdom, 2023.

Lord Northbourne. "Religion and Science." In *Science and the Myth of Progress*, edited by Mehrdad M. Zarandi, 77–92. Bloomington, IN: World Wisdom, 2003.

Nasr, Seyyed Hossein. *The Essential Seyyed Hossein Nasr*. Edited by William C. Chittick. Bloomington, IN: World Wisdom, 2007.

Nasr, Seyyed Hossein. *An Introduction to Islamic Cosmological Doctrines*. Cambridge, MA: Harvard University Press, 1964.

Nasr, Seyyed Hossein. *Islamic Philosophy from Its Origin to the Present: Philosophy in the Land of Prophecy*. Albany: State University of New York Press, 2006.

Nasr, Seyyed Hossein. *Knowledge and the Sacred*. Albany: State University of New York Press, 1989.

Nasr, Seyyed Hossein. *Man and Nature: The Spiritual Crisis in Modern Man*. Chicago: ABC International Group, 1997.

Nasr, Seyyed Hossein. *Religion and the Order of Nature*. New York: Oxford University Press, 1996.

Nasr, Seyyed Hossein. *A Sufi Commentary on the Tao Te Ching: The Way and Its Virtue*. Translated by Mohammad H. Faghfoory. Louisville: Fons Vitae, 2025.

Nasr, Seyyed Hossein. *Three Muslim Sages*. Cambridge, MA: Harvard University Press, 1964.

Nasr, Seyyed Hossein, Caner Dagli, Maria M. Dakake, Joseph E. B. Lumbard, and Mohammed Rustom, eds. *The Study Quran: A New Translation and Commentary*. New York: HarperOne, 2015.

Popper, Karl, and John C. Eccles. *The Self and Its Brain: An Argument for Interactionism*. New York: Routledge, 1983.

Rūmī, Jalāl al-Dīn. *Mathnawī-yi maʿnawī*. Edited by R. A. Nicholson. Tehran: Amīr Kabīr, 1978.

Saʿdī. *Gulistān*. Edited by Muḥammad Jawād Mashkūr. Tehran: Iqbāl, 1963.

Schuon, Frithjof. *The Essential Frithjof Schuon*. Edited by Seyyed Hossein Nasr. Bloomington, IN: World Wisdom, 2005.

Schuon, Frithjof. *From the Divine to the Human: Survey of Metaphysics and Epistemology*. Translated by Mark Perry and Jean-Pierre Lafouge. Bloomington, IN: World Wisdom, 2013.

Schuon, Frithjof. *Logic and Transcendence*. Translated by Peter N. Townsend. New York: Harper & Row, 1975.

Schuon, Frithjof. *Sufism: Veil and Quintessence*. Translated by Mark Perry, Jean-Pierre Lafouge, and James S. Cutsinger. Bloomington, IN: World Wisdom, 2006.

Index

www.ingramcontent.com/pod-product-compliance
Lightning Source LLC
Chambersburg PA
CBHW050537270326
41926CB00015B/3265